Traveling the Original Route 66

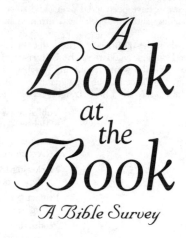

A
Look
at
the
Book

A Bible Survey

Bible Study Guide

From the Bible-teaching ministry of

Charles R. Swindoll

INSIGHT FOR LIVING

Chuck graduated in 1963 from Dallas Theological Seminary, where he now serves as the school's fourth president, helping to prepare a new generation of men and women for the ministry. Chuck has served in pastorates in three states: Massachusetts, Texas, and California, including almost twenty-three years at the First Evangelical Free Church in Fullerton, California. His sermon messages have been aired over radio since 1979 as the "Insight for Living" broadcast. A best-selling author, Chuck has written numerous books and booklets on many subjects.

This study guide is based on the outlines and transcripts of Chuck's sermons. Chapters 1–5 are coauthored by Lee Hough, a graduate of the University of Texas at Arlington and Dallas Theological Seminary. He also wrote the Living Insights sections for those chapters. Chapters 6–14 are coauthored by Bryce Klabunde, a graduate of Biola University and Dallas Theological Seminary. He also wrote the Living Insights sections for those chapters.

Editor in Chief:
Cynthia Swindoll

Coauthors of Text:
Lee Hough
Bryce Klabunde

Assistant Editor:
Wendy Peterson

Copy Editors:
Deborah Gibbs
Cheryl Gilmore
Glenda Schlahta

Designer:
Gary Lett

Publishing System Specialist:
Bob Haskins

Director, Communications Division:
Deedee Snyder

Marketing Manager:
Alene Cooper

Project Supervisor:
Kim Winburn

Production Manager:
John Norton

Printer:
Sinclair Printing Company

Unless otherwise identified, all Scripture references are from the New American Standard Bible, © The Lockman Foundation 1960, 1962, 1963, 1968, 1971, 1972, 1973, 1975, 1977. Used by permission.

The other translation cited is J. B. Phillips: The New Testament in Modern English [PHILLIPS].

An effort has been made to locate sources and obtain permission where necessary for the quotations used in this book. In the event of any unintentional omission, a modification will gladly be incorporated in future printings.

ISBN 0-8499-8494-7
Printed in the United States of America
COVER DESIGN: Nina Paris
COVER PHOTOGRAPH: SuperStock, Inc.
"God's Route 66" on page 9 is based on Route 66: The Mother Road by Michael Wallis (New York, N.Y.: St. Martin's Press, 1990).

CONTENTS

INTRODUCTION

One of the most famous (and I might add, nostalgic) journeys across America has recently received a lot of attention. It was an anniversary celebration of the old Route 66 that so many of us have driven. What a trip!

It occurred to me some time ago that there is a far more famous journey most have never taken—the *original* Route 66 through the Scriptures. Unfortunately, because this journey is so seldom traveled, relatively few people are aware of the scenery preserved by God.

We want to enjoy many of those things in this unique study. Our desire is to get an overview of the *whole* Word of God . . . a good look at the forest instead of each individual tree. I think you will find the journey fascinating.

So—have your Bible ready and your mind in gear. We're in for the time of our lives!

Chuck Swindoll

INTRODUCTION

PUTTING TRUTH
INTO ACTION

K nowledge apart from application falls short of God's desire for His children. He wants us to apply what we learn so that we will change and grow. This study guide was prepared with these goals in mind. As you go through the following pages, we hope your desire to discover biblical truth will grow as your understanding of God's Word increases and that you will be encouraged to apply what you've learned.

To assist you in your study, we've included a section called **Living Insights** at the end of each lesson. These exercises will challenge you to study further and to think of specific ways to put your discoveries into action.

On occasion a lesson is followed by a **Digging Deeper** section, which gives you additional information and resources to probe further into some issues raised in that lesson.

There are many ways to use this guide—in personal devotions, group studies, discussions with friends and family, and Sunday school classes. And, of course, it's an ideal study aid when you're listening to its corresponding "Insight for Living" radio series.

To benefit most from this study guide, we would encourage you to consider it a spiritual journal. That's why we've included space in the **Living Insights** for recording your thoughts and discoveries. We hope you'll return to those sections often for review and encouragement as you continue to grow in your walk with Christ.

Lee Hough
Coauthor of Text
Author of Living Insights

Bryce Klabunde
Coauthor of Text
Author of Living Insights

Traveling the Original Route 66

A Look at the Book

A Bible Survey

Chapter 1

THREE GATES THAT OPEN THE SCRIPTURES

Selected Scriptures

Once upon a time, the "Main Street" of America was Route 66. It stretched from Grant Park in Chicago to Santa Monica Boulevard and Ocean Avenue in Southern California—more than twenty-four hundred miles of concrete and asphalt that covered three time zones and eight states. Starting at Lake Michigan, you could travel west from Illinois to Missouri, through Kansas and Oklahoma, across Texas, into New Mexico, past Arizona, and, finally, dead-end at the roaring Pacific.

To see America, you traveled Route 66. To see the Bible, to gain a deeper understanding and appreciation of its terrain, you must travel the sixty-six books that stretch from Genesis to Revelation and span fifteen hundred years, forty generations, more than forty writers, and three different languages.

At one time or another, most Christians have traversed a stretch of the Bible's length. We've visited some of its more famous personalities and sites enough times that we know a verse or two by heart. A few of us can even give a detailed tour of an entire book or chapter. But explain how God's Route 66 fits together as a unit, or the manner in which all sixty-six books are laid out, and why? A simple quiz on such things would be passed by only a small minority. To most folks, the Bible remains a mental maze, a complex puzzle that defies understanding.

In this study, our goal is to gain an overall perspective of the Bible. We want to survey its entirety, understand its flow, note the unique way it was put together. Then we should be able to go back to the details with a deeper understanding of the magnificent story that unfolds page after page, book after book on God's Route 66.

1

Some Promised Benefits of Knowing the Bible

Route 66 always rewarded its travelers with several benefits, whether it was Ted Drewes' frozen custards in St. Louis, Missouri, or the Grand Canyon in northern Arizona. In the same way, God's original Route 66 also holds out rewards for its visitors. Psalm 119, for example, treats us to six.

1. In an impure world, God's Book will help you stay pure.

> How can a young man keep his way pure?
> By keeping it according to Thy word. . . .
> Thy word I have treasured in my heart,
> That I may not sin against Thee. (vv. 9, 11)

2. In a blind and confused world, God's Book will open your eyes.

> Open my eyes, that I may behold
> Wonderful things from Thy law. . . .
> Thy word is a lamp to my feet,
> And a light to my path. (vv. 18, 105)

3. In a self-centered, arrogant world, God's Book will produce a reverence for Him.

> Establish Thy word to Thy servant,
> As that which produces reverence for Thee. (v. 38)

4. In a world of heartache and affliction, God's Book will revive and renew your spirit.

> If Thy law had not been my delight,
> Then I would have perished in my affliction.
> I will never forget Thy precepts,
> For by them Thou hast revived me. (vv. 92–93)

5. In a world of hatred, ignorance, and misunderstanding, God's Book will make you wise, give insight, and provide understanding.

> O how I love Thy law!
> It is my meditation all the day.
> Thy commandments make me wiser than my enemies,
> For they are ever mine.
> I have more insight than all my teachers,
> For Thy testimonies are my meditation.
> I understand more than the aged,

2

Because I have observed Thy precepts.
(vv. 97–100; see also v. 24)

6. In a world of twisted perspectives, changing standards, and deceitful actions, God's Book will keep your mind clear.

I have restrained my feet from every evil way,
That I may keep Thy word.
I have not turned aside from Thine ordinances,
For Thou Thyself hast taught me. . . .
It is time for the Lord to act,
For they have broken Thy law.
Therefore I love Thy commandments
Above gold, yes, above fine gold.
Therefore I esteem right all Thy precepts
    concerning everything,
I hate every false way. (vv. 101–102, 126–128)

All of these benefits are wonderful, but will they last? America's Route 66 has been closed, and now weeds grow in the wrinkled cracks of this aged highway's discarded stretches. Can the same thing happen to the Bible? Will its unique benefits one day cease because it, too, has become outdated? The prophet Isaiah reassures us this will never happen.

The grass withers, the flower fades,
But the word of our God stands forever. (Isa. 40:8)

All Who Wish to Know Must Pass through These "Gates"

Before we begin our journey from Eden to the end times, we must first pass through three gates. Each one, as it is opened and understood, will increase our confidence in the reliability of God's Book. So it is crucial that we study each of them carefully.

Gate 1: The Doctrine of Revelation

This has to do with God revealing His truths to His people. How? Basically, the Lord used three methods. First, and most common, He *spoke* directly to individuals.

The Lord spoke to Moses in the wilderness of Sinai. (Num. 1:1a)

Now it came about after the death of Moses the

3

servant of the Lord that the Lord spoke to Joshua the son of Nun. (Josh. 1:1a)

Second, God *illustrated* His revelation. The apostle John, for example, was given a prophetic vision and then told,

"Write therefore the things which you have seen, and the things which are, and the things which shall take place after these things." (Rev. 1:19)

And third, God personally *wrote* His truths.

"These words the Lord spoke to all your assembly at the mountain from the midst of the fire, of the cloud and of the thick gloom, with a great voice, and He added no more. And He wrote them on two tablets of stone and gave them to me." (Deut. 5:22; see also 4:13)

These three methods of revelation cover most but not all of the ways God revealed His truth. In some cases, the means are simply not explained, as in Galatians 1:11–12, where the apostle Paul states:

For I would have you know, brethren, that the gospel which was preached by me is not according to man. For I neither received it from man, nor was I taught it, but I received it through a revelation of Jesus Christ.

Regardless of the method, the act of revelation was always the same: *a supernatural work of God in which He communicated divine truth to human beings that they otherwise would not or could not know.* Does He still do this today? Some self-appointed, modern-day prophets claim that He does. The Bible itself, however, says no. Jude 3, for example, categorically states,

Beloved, while I was making every effort to write you about our common salvation, I felt the necessity to write to you appealing that you contend earnestly for the faith which was once for all delivered to the saints.

Notice that "the faith"—the body of truth known as God's revelation—has been deposited "once for all" into the hands of God's people. The transaction is finished. We no longer need nor should we look for divine messages revealing new information. All

4

that's needed for faith and practice has already been given (see 2 Tim. 3:16–17).

Gate 2: The Doctrine of Inspiration

The doctrine of inspiration has to do with the writers of Scripture *receiving* and *recording* God's truths accurately. Many Christians are confused about this doctrine because they don't understand the biblical meaning behind the word *inspiration*. When people applaud an artist's work as inspired, they're not saying it is without error or the result of some supernatural act of God. But when that same word is used of the Scriptures, that's exactly what we mean. By our definition, then, inspiration is:

> *The supernatural act of God whereby He so directed human authors of Scripture that, without destroying their individuality, literary style, or personality, His complete and connected thought toward humanity was received/recorded without error or contradiction—each word being supernaturally written and preserved so as to result in an infallible document in the original writings.*

That's quite a mouthful of theological jargon! Let's simplify what's being said by examining this doctrine's six basic components. First, the *cause:* God the Holy Spirit.

> No prophecy was ever made by an act of human will, but men *moved by the Holy Spirit* spoke from God. (2 Pet. 1:21, emphasis added)

Second, the *agent:* A human writer (v. 21b). God used sinful, fallible individuals to record His infallible Word.

Third, the *result:* An inerrant document revealed by God and thoroughly accredited.

> All Scripture is inspired by God and profitable for teaching, for reproof, for correction, for training in righteousness; that the man of God may be adequate, equipped for every good work. (2 Tim. 3:16–17)

Fourth, the *source:* God Himself (2 Pet. 1:21c).

Fifth, the *process:* God moved through human beings, and they, apart from anything unique in themselves, recorded His truth completely free from error. The Greek term for *moved* in 2 Peter 1:21 signifies that the authors of Scripture were "'borne along,' or impelled,

5

by the Holy Spirit's power, not acting according to their own wills, or simply expressing their own thoughts, but expressing the mind of God in words provided and ministered by Him."[1]

Sixth, the *extent*: Inspiration extends to both the Old and New Testaments with no part being more or less inspired than any other. In 1 Timothy 5:18, for example, Paul writes, "For the Scripture says, 'You shall not muzzle the ox while he is threshing,' and 'The laborer is worthy of his wages.'" Here Paul quotes an Old Testament law alongside Jesus' words and labels them both "Scripture" (see Deut. 25:4; Luke 10:7). The Greek term for this word is *graphē*, and it is only used of the inspired writings of the Bible.

Combine all six elements, and perhaps now you can appreciate as never before the exciting uniqueness the doctrine of inspiration conveys about the Bible. But remember this too: Inspiration in the biblical sense no longer occurs. It stands to reason that if revelation has ceased, so has inspiration.

Gate 3: The Doctrine of Illumination

Illumination has to do with our *understanding* and *applying* the Scriptures.

> "But when He, the Spirit of truth, comes, He will guide you into all the truth; for He will not speak on His own initiative, but whatever He hears, He will speak; and He will disclose to you what is to come." (John 16:13)

That's the work of illumination: *the supernatural influence of the Holy Spirit upon all who are in right relation with God to comprehend and apply inspired truths.* Paul underscores this same doctrine in his first epistle to the Corinthians.

> Just as it is written,
> "Things which eye has not seen and ear has not heard,
> And which have not entered the heart of man,
> All that God has prepared for those who love Him."

---

1. W. E. Vine, *Vine's Expository Dictionary of New Testament Words* (McClean, Va.: MacDonald Publishing Co., n.d.), p. 771.

For to us God revealed them through the Spirit; for the Spirit searches all things, even the depths of God. . . . We have received, not the spirit of the world, but the Spirit who is from God, that we might know the things freely given to us by God, which things we also speak, not in words taught by human wisdom, but in those taught by the Spirit, combining spiritual thoughts with spiritual words. But a natural man does not accept the things of the Spirit of God; for they are foolishness to him, and he cannot understand them, because they are spiritually appraised. But he who is spiritual appraises all things. . . . We have the mind of Christ. (1 Cor. 2:9–16)

Notice the contrast Paul draws between the natural man's *inability* and the spiritual man's *ability*. The natural man (1) "does not accept" (*dechomai*—"welcome" in the Greek) God's truths and (2) "cannot understand" them (*ginōskō*—"know by experience"). This explains why the unsaved fail to grasp or appreciate the wisdom of Scripture. The spiritual person, on the other hand, has the Spirit to illumine his or her mind, "that we might know the things freely given to us by God."

Since new revelation is no longer being recorded and preserved, God takes what has already been revealed and makes it known to us through His Spirit. The gate of illumination, unlike revelation and inspiration, is still open. Even now, His Spirit is at work in you, teaching, convicting, illuminating! Kind of exciting, isn't it?

The Practical Value of These Three Truths

Bible doctrine, to many people, is nothing more than esoteric mumblings of monks and boring seminary professors. It's dead, impractical, ancient history, they say.

To show just how wrong they are, let's close this study with three statements, each beginning the same way, that highlight the practical side of revelation, inspiration, and illumination.

- If God had not given us His revelation, we would live our lives in spiritual ignorance.

No standard	No knowledge	No assurance
No victory over evil	No direction	No hope

- If God had not protected His revelation from error, the Bible would be an unreliable book of no greater value than any other literature written by fallible human beings.

- If God did not open our eyes and hearts, we would neither understand His purposes nor know His will. We would have no comfort, no relief, no direction.

 Living Insights

Dubbed "The Mother Road" by John Steinbeck, Route 66 weaved its wayfarers through a giant patchwork of Americana. Colorful places like Two Guns, Arizona; Meramec Caverns, Missouri; and the Wigwam Village in Rialto, California, rose to meet travelers around every bend. From her shoulders spread a view of amber waves of grain, purple mountain majesties, fruited plains. Mile after mile, she showed you the very essence of America the beautiful, the land and its people.

How much of the Bible's Route 66 are you familiar with? Can you reconstruct its layout by naming the individual books in their consecutive order, starting with Genesis and running all the way across nine "regions" to Revelation? Try charting out as much as you can on the map on the facing page. We've provided the name of the first book in each category. See if you can fill in the rest. Happy motoring!

 Living Insights

> "Enter by the narrow gate; for the gate is wide, and the way is broad that leads to destruction, and many are those who enter by it. For the gate is small, and the way is narrow that leads to life, and few are those who find it." (Matt. 7:13–14)

How confident are you that the road to righteousness revealed in the Bible is reliable? Some have said there are many roads that lead to God. Faithful Buddhists have their own path, as do Muslims and Mormons, and they all lead, supposedly, to the same place—enlightenment, nirvana, heaven.

(Continued on page 10)

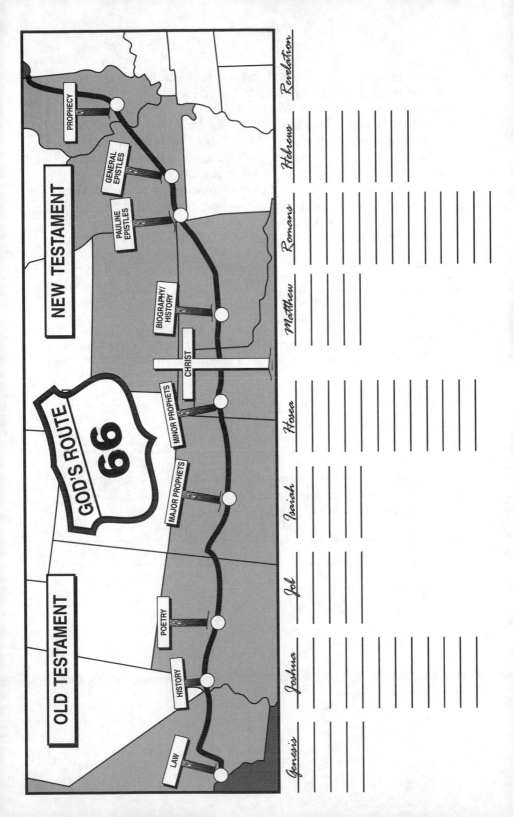

The problem, of course, is that Jesus Himself denied any such notion of another road to salvation with emphatic declarations like, "I am the way, and the truth, and the life; no one comes to the Father, but through Me" (John 14:6). To deny that He said it or that it's true would be a direct attack on the reliability of the Scriptures. And if the Scriptures can't be trusted, then who's to say what's true and what isn't and by what authority?

Suppose someone said they believed in Jesus but not in all that hocus-pocus about His being born of a virgin or casting out demons. How would you respond, using one or more of the doctrines discussed in the chapter?

_____

_____

_____

Let's try another. What would you say to someone who believed the Bible is full of errors because it was written by fallible human beings?

_____

_____

_____

Last, respond to the person who says the Bible is an inspired piece of literature in the same way that the Koran or Buddha's Four Noble Truths are.

_____

_____

_____

Chapter 2

A LOOK AT THE BOOK
Selected Scriptures

Bible. Coffee thermos. Jackets. Camera. Twelve rolls of film. Fishing poles. Four boxes of Hostess Twinkies . . .

Oh, hello there! I was just running down the list of a few essentials I thought we might need on our road trip through the Scriptures. Let's see . . . swim trunks. Tennis racquets. Hiking boots. What? Right, binoculars, good idea. Isn't this going to be great? If you want to get really excited, read what the famous evangelist Billy Sunday wrote about his travels along God's Route 66.

> Twenty-nine years ago, with the Holy Spirit as my Guide, I entered at the portico of Genesis, walked down the corridor of the Old Testament art-galleries, where pictures of Noah, Abraham, Moses, Joseph, Isaac, Jacob, and Daniel hang on the wall. I passed into the music room of the Psalms where the spirit sweeps the keyboard of nature until it seems that every reed and pipe in God's great organ responds to the harp of David the sweet singer of Israel.
>
> I entered the chamber of Ecclesiastes, where the voice of the preacher is heard, and into the conservatory of Sharon and the lily of the valley where sweet spices filled and perfumed my life.
>
> I entered the business office of Proverbs and on into the observatory of the prophets where I saw telescopes of various sizes pointing to far off events, concentrating on the bright and morning Star which was to rise above the moonlit hills of Judea for our salvation and redemption.
>
> I entered the audience room of the King of kings, catching a vision written by Matthew, Mark, Luke, and John. Thence into the correspondence room with Paul, Peter, James and John writing their Epistles.
>
> I stepped into the throne room of Revelation where tower the glittering peaks, where sits the King of kings upon His throne of glory with the healing of the nations in His hand, and I cried out:

11

All hail the power of Jesus' name!
Let angels prostrate fall;
Bring forth the royal diadem
And crown Him Lord of all.[1]

Isn't that a beautiful personal travelogue? If we want to look back on our tour of the Bible with the same understanding and awe, then we'll need to pack more than just our toothbrushes and sunscreen. We'll need to bring along a thorough understanding of the route we're about to take, so let's continue preparing for our excursion through the Scriptures, this time examining some of the unique features of God's Route 66.

The Name: Bible

It may surprise some of you to know that the word *Bible* does not appear anywhere in the sixty-six books of God's revelation. Yet it is the most familiar term people use to refer to Scripture. So where did the name come from? A plant. No, really, it's true. In ancient times the most common "paper" used was a reed that grew in the lakes and rivers of Egypt and Syria called *papyrus*. The Greek name for the fibrous outer coat or bark of the papyrus, which was the part actually written on, was called *biblos*. The plural form, *biblia*, came to mean "writings" or "rolls"—a designation for the rolled-up scrolls so common in antiquity. As early as the second century A.D., Christians began using *biblia* to refer to the sacred books of Scripture.[2]

The Divisions: Two Testaments

Another important distinction of the Bible is its layout. I can still remember how quickly I got lost on God's Route 66 in my first Bible study as a young Christian.[3] I was with about four others and the leader asked us to turn to the book of John. Book of John? I wondered. What book? All I had was my Bible. Meanwhile, as I

---

1. Billy Sunday, as quoted by W. A. Criswell in *Why I Preach That the Bible Is Literally True* (Nashville, Tenn.: Broadman Press, 1969), pp. 99–100.

2. See Merrill F. Unger, *Unger's Bible Dictionary*, 3d ed. (Chicago, Ill.: Moody Press, 1966), pp. 143–44. The term *biblos* is used for "book" in Luke 4:17: "And the book of the prophet Isaiah was handed to Him. And He opened the book, and found the place where it was written" (see also v. 20; 20:42; Mark 12:26).

3. This is coauthor Lee Hough's experience.

sat there panicking, everyone else quickly thumbed their way to the juncture of John's gospel in the New Testament.

What I didn't understand, of course, is that even though the Bible is considered one book, it is actually made up of sixty-six individual books divided into two major divisions—the Old and New Testaments.

> The word "testament" means "covenant," or agreement. The Old Testament is the covenant God made with man about his salvation before Christ came. The New Testament is the agreement God made with man about his salvation after Christ came.
>
> In the Old Testament, we find the covenant of law. In the New Testament, we find the covenant of grace which came through Jesus Christ. One led into the other (Galatians 3:17–25).
>
> The Old commences what the New completes.
> The Old gathers around Sinai,
> The New around Calvary.
> The Old is associated with Moses,
> The New with Christ (John 1:17). . . .
> From Adam to Abraham we have the history of the human race.
> From Abraham to Christ we have the history of the chosen race.
> From Christ on we have the history of the Church.[4]

The Process: How Did We Get Our Bible?

The Old Testament was originally written in Hebrew with a few short passages in Aramaic. But Koine (common) Greek was the verbal vehicle through which the inspired authors laid down God's revelation in the New Testament. Since then, the divine Route 66 has been "repaved," so to speak, time and again. That is, it has been copied and translated into hundreds of different languages. Do any of the original writings still exist? No. So how do we know the copy we have today still follows the same route as the original? I'm glad

---

4. Henrietta C. Mears, *What the Bible Is All About* (Minneapolis, Minn.: Billy Graham Evangelistic Association, 1966), pp. 1–2.

you asked. Because, by uncovering the answer to that important question we will discover still another unique feature of the Bible.

Christians don't claim to possess the original manuscripts of the Scriptures. We do claim, however, that we have some *very accurate copies!* To illustrate this, suppose you have an old photograph of your grandfather that's beginning to fade and crack. To preserve the original, you have a copy made, a duplicate just like the original. Now, technically speaking, it's not the actual photograph taken of your grandfather, but it is just like the original and you have every confidence in referring to it as your grandfather's picture.

In the same way, we have every confidence in referring to our Bible as an accurate copy of the original. How do we know? First, the process of copying was done with unbelievable patience and incredible accuracy. Consider, for example, the strict code followed by the Talmudists (A.D. 100–500) for translating synagogue scrolls.

[1] A synagogue roll must be written on the skins of clean animals, [2] prepared for the particular use of the synagogue by a Jew. [3] These must be fastened together with strings taken from clean animals. [4] Every skin must contain a certain number of columns, equal throughout the entire codex. [5] The length of each column must not extend over less than 48 or more than 60 lines; and the breadth must consist of thirty letters. [6] The whole copy must be first-lined; and if three words be written without a line, it is worthless. [7] The ink should be black, neither red, green, nor any other colour, and be prepared according to a definite recipe. [8] An authentic copy must be the exemplar, from which the transcriber ought not in the least deviate. [9] No word or letter, not even a yod, must be written from memory, the scribe not having looked at the codex before him . . . [10] Between every consonant the space of a hair or thread must intervene; [11] between every new parashah, or section, the breadth of nine consonants; [12] between every book, three lines. [13] The fifth book of Moses must terminate exactly with a line; but the rest need not do so. [14] Besides this, the copyist must sit in full Jewish dress, [15] wash his whole body, [16] not begin to

write the name of God with a pen newly dipped in ink, [17] and should a king address him while writing that name he must take no notice of him.[5]

This is but one example of the meticulous methods transcribers employed for centuries in copying the Scriptures by hand. Still another reassurance of having an accurate copy of the Bible's hand-written originals is the abundance of manuscript evidence.

There are now more than 5,300 known Greek manuscripts of the New Testament. Add over 10,000 Latin Vulgate and at least 9,300 other early versions (MSS) and we have more than 24,000 manuscript copies of portions of the New Testament in existence today.[6]

Sir Frederic Kenyon, one of the greatest authorities in the field of New Testament textual criticism, adds:

Scholars are satisfied that they possess substantially the true text of the principal Greek and Roman writers whose works have come down to us, of Sophocles, of Thucydides, of Cicero, of Virgil; yet our knowledge of their writings depends on a mere handful of manuscripts, whereas the manuscripts of the New Testament are counted by hundreds, and even thousands.[7]

What does this wealth of manuscript material reveal? Kenyon explains, "The Christian can take the whole Bible in his hand and say without fear or hesitation that he holds in it the true Word of God, handed down without essential loss from generation to generation throughout the centuries."[8]

5. Samuel Davidson, as quoted by Josh McDowell in *Evidence That Demands a Verdict*, rev. ed. (San Bernardino, Calif.: Here's Life Publishers, 1979), p. 53.

6. McDowell, *Evidence That Demands a Verdict*, p. 39.

7. Sir Frederic Kenyon, as quoted by McDowell in *Evidence That Demands a Verdict*, p. 45.

8. Kenyon, as quoted by McDowell in *Evidence That Demands a Verdict*, p. 53. Speaking of the differences between various of the Old Testament manuscripts, Gleason Archer attested that "none of them affects a single doctrine of Scripture." As for the New Testament, Benjamin Warfield concluded, "Such has been the providence of God in preserving for His Church in each and every age a competently exact text of the Scriptures," pp. 45–46.

The Contents: Sections within the Testaments

Now let's briefly review the eight major divisions along God's Route 66, four in the Old Testament and four in the New.

The Old Testament

1. Genesis through Deuteronomy. The first five books fall under the category known as the *Law*. In this section, Moses traces the beginning of all things and the formation of the nation Israel, through which God revealed His rules for righteous living.

2. Joshua through Esther. This twelve-book stretch of the Old Testament is known as the *historical* section. Here we follow Israel from her entrance into the Promised Land, through her days with judges and kings, and into and out of bondage to foreign, pagan nations.

3. Job through Song of Solomon. These five books form the *poetical* section. The name is derived from the style of Hebrew that David and Solomon used in writing most of these books.

4. Isaiah through Malachi. This section is made up of the *prophetical* books. Normally, they are divided into two parts, the major prophets (Isaiah through Daniel) and the minor prophets (Hosea through Malachi). The distinction comes from the size of the books, not the content.

The New Testament

1. Matthew through John. The first section of the New Testament is *biographical* in nature. It traces the life of Jesus Christ from His birth to His resurrection, covering the events from the viewpoint of each writer.

2. Acts. This is a *historical* account of the growth of the church from Pentecost to Paul's arrest in Rome. In chapters 1–12, Peter is the main character; and then in chapters 13–28, Paul becomes the central figure.

3. Romans through Jude. Known as the *doctrinal* section, this portion of God's route sets forth the finer points of Christian truth in twenty-one letters authored by five different men.

4. Revelation. This is the major *prophetical* book of the New Testament. It unveils and outlines God's plans for the future of Israel, the Gentile nations, and this earth.

The Theme: The Lord Jesus Christ

The last unique feature for us to become familiar with is the Bible's unifying theme. To fully appreciate the miraculous nature of its unity, we would do well to pause and consider, with Josh McDowell's help, some of its diversity.

Here is a book:

1. Written over a 1,500 year span.
2. Written over 40 generations.
3. Written by over 40 authors from every walk of life . . . :
   Moses, a political leader, trained in the universities of Egypt
   Peter, a fisherman
   Amos, a herdsman
   Joshua, a military general
   Nehemiah, a cupbearer
   Daniel, a prime minister
   Luke, a doctor
   Solomon, a king
   Matthew, a tax collector
   Paul, a rabbi
4. Written in different places:
   Moses in the wilderness
   Jeremiah in a dungeon
   Daniel on a hillside and in a palace
   Paul inside prison walls
   Luke while traveling
   John on the isle of Patmos
   Others in the rigors of a military campaign
5. Written at different times:
   David in times of war
   Solomon in times of peace
6. Written during different moods:
   Some writing from the heights of joy and others writing from the depths of sorrow and despair
7. Written on three continents:

Asia, Africa, and Europe[9]

Despite this incredible diversity, the Bible still possesses a singular theme threaded throughout its entirety that extols the Lord Jesus Christ. The Old Testament looks forward to Him and the New Testament looks back. The Old prepares us for Him through figures, symbols, and predictions, and the New portrays and explains Him as their complete fulfillment. The Old glimpses His shadow; the New reveals His substance.

Jesus affirmed this as He conversed with the two men on the road to Emmaus after His resurrection.

> "Was it not necessary for the Christ to suffer these things and to enter into His glory?" And beginning with Moses and with all the prophets, He explained to them the things concerning Himself in all the Scriptures. (Luke 24:26–27)

Not long afterwards, Jesus appeared to His disciples in Jerusalem and again reminded them of how the Scriptures point to Him.

> "These are My words which I spoke to you while I was still with you, that all things which are written about Me in the Law of Moses and the Prophets and the Psalms must be fulfilled." Then He opened their minds to understand the Scriptures, and He said to them, "Thus it is written, that the Christ should suffer and rise again from the dead the third day." (vv. 44–46; see also John 5:39)

As J. B. Fowler, Jr. said, "Christ is the crimson thread that holds all the Scriptures together."

> In Genesis, He is the Seed of the woman.
> In Exodus, He's the Passover Lamb.
> In Leviticus, He is the atoning Sacrifice.
> In Numbers, He is the bronze Serpent.
> In Deuteronomy, He's the promised Prophet.
> In Joshua, He is the unseen Captain.
> In Judges, He is my Deliverer.
> In Ruth, He's my heavenly Kinsman.

9. McDowell, *Evidence That Demands a Verdict*, p. 16. For further study, we recommend this book of McDowell's and *The Symphony of Scripture*, by Mark Strom (Downers Grove, Ill.: InterVarsity Press, 1990).

In Samuel, Kings, and Chronicles, He is the
    promised King.
In Ezra and Nehemiah, He's the Restorer of the
    nation.
In Esther, He is my Advocate.
In Job, my Redeemer.
In Psalms, He is my All in All.
In Proverbs, my Pattern.
In Ecclesiastes, my Goal.
In Song of Solomon, my Beloved.
In the prophets, He is the coming Prince of Peace.
In Matthew, He is the King.
In Mark, the Servant.
In Luke, the Son of Man.
In John, the Son of God.
In Acts, He is risen, seated, and sending.
In the letters, He is indwelling and filling.
And in Revelation, He is returning and reigning.[10]

He is the King of the Scriptures, the King of the road . . . the
straight and narrow road to heaven.

 Living Insights   STUDY ONE

As we noted at the close of our chapter, Christ is the unifying
theme throughout the Bible. Let's pause now for a more in-depth
look at how the Passover lamb, the bronze serpent, and some
institutions and events in the Old Testament foreshadow His person
and work. Take a moment to carefully read each passage listed; then
make as many comparisons to Christ and His work of redemption
as you can in the space provided.

Israel's exodus from Egypt and crossing the Red Sea
(Exod. 13:17–14:31; John 5:24; 2 Cor. 5:17)

_____

_____

_____

10. Adapted from *Illustrating Great Words of the New Testament*, by J. B. Fowler, Jr. (Nashville,
Tenn.: Broadman Press, 1991), p. 98.

The Passover lamb
(Exod. 12:1–14; John 1:28–29; 1 Cor. 5:7; 1 Pet. 1:17–19)

_____

_____

_____

The bronze serpent
(Num. 21:4–10; John 3:14–15)

_____

_____

_____

Jonah's experience with the great fish
(Jon. 1:1–2:10; Matt. 12:38–41)

_____

_____

_____

Can you draw any other parallels between the Old Testament and Christ? Use the following space to write down the comparisons that come to mind.

_____

_____

_____

_____

_____

_____

_____

_____

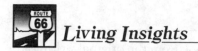

Embedded in prophecies, woven through analogies, and tucked into types, Christ permeates the Old Testament. In the Gospels, though, He parades in full view, only to disappear into the clouds at the end. Over in Acts and the Epistles, He reaches down from heaven into the hearts of His disciples who carry His touch to the world. Finally, in Revelation, He gallops into full view again, this time as the conquering King of Kings.

The Bible exudes Christ . . . but do our lives? Is there a parallel between our lifestyle and His that is plainly visible to others? Perhaps all of us could point to specific deeds done in the distant past that heralded Christ's person and work of salvation. But what about recently? What about at the office yesterday or in the normal routines of home this past week? Think about that for a moment, and then note the specific ways your actions, not your words, have revealed Christ.

Digging Deeper

Following the course the Bible took from the original writings to today's English translations is an interesting side trip. If you choose to explore this route someday, we recommend that you take along *The Complete Guide to Bible Versions*, by Philip Wesley Comfort (Wheaton, Ill.: Tyndale House Publishers, Living Books, 1991). The following chart of Bible versions previews some of the fascinating stops you'll make along the way.

Ancient Writings

Ancient Translations

Jerome's Translation (the Latin Vulgate)	400
Wycliffe's English Translation	1382
Tyndale's Translation	1525
Coverdale's Translation	1535
The Great Bible	1539
Geneva Bible	1560
Bishops' Bible	1568
King James Version (The Authorized Version)	1611
American Standard Version	1901
Revised Standard Version	1952
The New American Standard Bible	1971
The New International Version	1978
The New King James Version	1982

Many Modern Translations and Paraphrases

Chapter 3

THE FLOW OF BIBLICAL HISTORY: HIS STORY

Selected Scriptures

In its heyday, Route 66 entertained its patrons with many attractions—like Lincoln's tomb, the George Washington Carver monument, the Will Rogers Memorial in Claremore, Oklahoma, and the Palo Duro Canyon in Amarillo, Texas. Further west you could walk through a petrified forest, see the Painted Desert, or gawk at the Grand Canyon and Hoover Dam. The road was a continuous cornucopia of interesting people, places, and things that never left any two of its travelers with exactly the same impression.

Whichever way one toured America's Main Street, the sights and sounds encountered along the way left an indelible map of memories in each person's mind. One they could follow at any time, anywhere, and always retrace their journey across the entire width of America's heartland on the Mother Road.

Is there such a personalized map in your mind of God's Route 66? Can you trace your way from Genesis to Revelation? Do you know the important events, landmarks, or people that belong to each major section of the Bible's inspired path? In this chapter, we want to consider four memorable ways to tour the Scriptures—four different paths for traveling the same road so you, too, will always be able to find your way across the entire width of human history on the straight and narrow road of God's Word.

Various Ways to Journey through the Scriptures

The focus of our first tour will be people.

Remembering Significant Individuals

In the Old Testament, it's easy to flag each book in your mind by tracing the key people.

Genesis: Adam and Eve, Cain and Abel, Noah, Abraham, Isaac, Jacob, Joseph.

Exodus/Leviticus/Numbers/Deuteronomy: Moses.

Joshua: Joshua and Caleb.

Judges: Deborah, Barak, Gideon, Jephthah, Samson.

Ruth: Ruth.

1 and 2 Samuel: Eli, Samuel, Saul, David.

1 and 2 Kings/1 and 2 Chronicles: Solomon, followed by a procession of kings and prophets of Israel's divided kingdom.

Then a series of books that each bear the name of its significant individual: Ezra, Nehemiah, Esther, Job.

Psalms: David.

Proverbs/Ecclesiastes/Song of Solomon: Solomon.

Isaiah: Isaiah.

Jeremiah/Lamentations: Jeremiah.

Next, the books of the prophets, which all bear the name of their authors: Ezekiel, Daniel, Hosea, Joel, Amos, Obadiah, Jonah, Micah, Nahum, Habakkuk, Zephaniah, Haggai, Zechariah, Malachi.

Finally, when Malachi's pen is still, a four-hundred-year period of silence ensues. Then Jesus Christ, obviously the most important figure of the New Testament, ushers in a new era. Other key individuals are John the Baptizer and Jesus' twelve disciples, some of whom authored portions of the New Testament.

- Peter led the early church and wrote the two letters bearing his name.

- John wrote one of the four gospels, three letters, and Revelation.

- Paul wrote all but eight of the New Testament epistles; and much of the book of Acts chronicles his early missionary journeys.

- James and Jude wrote letters bearing their names.

Tracing Important Events

Another way to tour the Bible is to note important events. An overview of some of them is provided in the chart on the following page. These events are marked in bold, and they are seen in relation to the scriptural books you'll find them in.

Observing the Hebrew People

A third way to create a memorable trip through the Bible is to follow God's chosen people, the Jews. Our starting point for this journey is Genesis 12, where God promises to make a great nation of Abraham's offspring, Isaac. Through his son Jacob, the Hebrew population flourished, and under the last patriarch, Joseph, the fledgling nation resettled in Egypt. The Egyptians later felt threatened by Israel's growth, so they enslaved her people for four hundred

SURVEY CHART OF THE BIBLE BOOKS

Creation, Fall, Flood, Babel,
Patriarchs, Bondage,
Deliverance, Law,
Wanderings,
Conquest of Canaan
and Compromise

Samuel, Saul,
David, Solomon

United
Kingdom

Northern (Israel)

Invasion by Assyria
(722 B.C.)

Between the Testaments—400 Silent Years
(No Scripture written)

Apostles and
Beginning of Church
Missions

John the Baptizer
Lord Jesus Christ
Disciples

Returns

1. Zerubbabel
2. Ezra
3. Nehemiah

and
Restoration

Exile in Babylon
(586 B.C.–516 B.C.)

Divided
Kingdom

1 Kings 12–
2 Chronicles 36

Southern (Judah)

Books:
Jonah
Amos
Hosea

Books:
Genesis (Beginnings)
Job (Suffering)
Exodus (Deliverance)
Leviticus (Worship)
Numbers (Wanderings)
Deuteronomy (Remember)
Joshua (Conquest)
Judges (Defeat)
Ruth (Love)

Books:
1 Samuel 1–1 Kings 11
Psalms, Proverbs
Ecclesiastes and
Song of Solomon

Books of the Prophets:

Preexilic
Obadiah
Joel
Isaiah
Micah

Nahum
Habakkuk
Zephaniah
Jeremiah

Exilic
Lamentations
Ezekiel
Daniel

Postexilic
Haggai
Zechariah
Malachi
Other Books
Ezra
Nehemiah
Esther

Books:
Matthew (King)
Mark (Servant)
Luke (Man)
John (God)
Acts
Epistles
Revelation

25

years. God then sent Moses to lead Israel out of Egypt, through the wilderness wanderings, and to the border of the Promised Land. During the time of affluence that followed, the history of the Hebrews is best described by the following vicious cycle:

From bondage to spiritual faith
From spiritual faith to great courage
From great courage to liberty
From liberty to abundance
From abundance to selfishness
From selfishness to complacency
From complacency to spiritual apathy
From spiritual apathy to indulgence
From indulgence to dependency
From dependency to bondage

After their final deliverance from this monotonous cycle, Israel demanded a king and was given Saul, who was succeeded by David and then his son Solomon. Under Solomon's son, Israel split into two kingdoms, the north (Israel) and the south (Judah), and the leadership in both was generally wicked. Finally, in 722 B.C., the northern kingdom was overrun, and in 586 B.C., the southern kingdom fell.

Following a lengthy exile in Babylon and Persia, the Jews were allowed to return to their land and, once again, become a nation. Like all other peoples, they fought to keep their sovereignty, but Rome came to power and eventually dominated them. It was during this time that Jesus arrived on the scene, but the Jews rejected Him as their Messiah. The Savior, however, has not forgotten His people, as Paul reminds us in Romans 11:1:

> I say then, God has not rejected His people, has He? May it never be! For I too am an Israelite, a descendant of Abraham, of the tribe of Benjamin.

Understanding the Centrality of Christ

Still another way to trace your way through the Scriptures is by noting the centrality of Christ. You can begin in Genesis, where God says:

> "And I will put enmity
> Between you and the woman,
> And between your seed and her seed;
> He shall bruise you on the head,

26

And you shall bruise him on the heel." (3:15)

The Lord is picturing for us the inevitable future conflict between His Son and Satan for our souls. One day, He says, Satan
will bruise Christ with the suffering of the Cross, and Jesus, in turn,
will destroy Satan with the victory of the Resurrection. This glimpse
in Genesis is the beginning of His story of redemption that is woven
throughout biblical history. Remember it this way: Concerning the
coming, ministry, death, and resurrection of Christ,

- the Old Testament looks forward,

- the Gospels look at, and

- the letters look back.

Several Biblical Statements of Reassurance

No matter which sight-seeing tour you take through the Bible,
God's sovereign hand in orchestrating our redemption is unmistak-
ably clear. History is not just random events careening off one
another in a pointless vacuum of purposelessness. It is His story,
His loving plan of saving a prodigal world from its own destruction.
Paul touches on this in his letter to the Colossians.

> For [God] delivered us from the domain of darkness,
> and transferred us to the kingdom of His beloved
> Son, in whom we have redemption, the forgiveness
> of sins. And He is the image of the invisible God,
> the firstborn of all creation. For by Him all things
> were created, both in the heavens and on earth, vis-
> ible and invisible, whether thrones or dominions or
> rulers or authorities—all things have been created
> by Him and for Him. And He is before all things,
> and in Him all things hold together. (1:13–17)

Paul also spoke of God's sovereign purpose in Athens at the
Areopagus. Listen to his words.

> "The God who made the world and all things in it,
> since He is Lord of heaven and earth, does not dwell
> in temples made with hands; neither is He served
> by human hands, as though He needed anything,
> since He Himself gives to all life and breath and all
> things; and He made from one, every nation of

mankind to live on all the face of the earth, having determined their appointed times, and the boundaries of their habitation, that they should seek God, if perhaps they might grope for Him and find Him, though He is not far from each one of us; for in Him we live and move and exist, as even some of your own poets have said, 'For we also are His offspring.' Being then the offspring of God, we ought not to think that the Divine nature is like gold or silver or stone, an image formed by the art and thought of man. Therefore having overlooked the times of ignorance, God is now declaring to men that all everywhere should repent, because He has fixed a day in which He will judge the world in righteousness through a Man whom He has appointed, having furnished proof to all men by raising Him from the dead." (Acts 17:24–31)

Last, consider the testimony King Nebuchadnezzar gave concerning God's sovereignty the moment his reason returned after he had been humbled for his pride.

> "And all the inhabitants of the earth are
>   accounted as nothing,
> But He does according to His will in the host of
>   heaven
> And among the inhabitants of earth;
> And no one can ward off His hand
> Or say to Him, 'What hast Thou done?'"
> (Dan. 4:35)

Whether or not the world acknowledges His dominion, God is in control of the events that happen on earth. Nothing transpires outside the parameters of His story for humankind.

According to "His Story," Where Are You?

If you were to plot your position in His story as we've traced it through the Scriptures, where would you be? Are you still looking for the Messiah, like the Hebrews in the Old Testament? Have you rejected Christ, like the Jews in the days of the New Testament? Or are you like the faithful remnant who did trust in God's Son and did find their place in His plan?

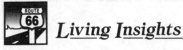 *Living Insights*

Such a lot of ground we've covered! Now, before you run out of gas trying to journey any farther down God's Route 66, pull over and refresh your memory with what you've just learned. We'll give you a significant individual, an important event, some unique part of Hebrew history, or a glimpse of the centrality of Christ, and you write down which book or grouping of books of the Bible you would find it in. And lock your map in the glove compartment. No fair peeking until you're through!

If I wanted to learn about . . .	I would look in . . .
Noah	_____
the Creation	_____
the history of the early church	_____
Israel's deliverance from Egypt	_____
John the Baptizer	_____
the Seed of the woman	_____
the wilderness wanderings	_____
David's reign	_____
the patriarchs	_____
the Fall of the human race	_____
the disciples	_____
the divided kingdom	_____
Israel's return and restoration	_____
Jesus' earthly life	_____

 Living Insights

How would you chart the history of God's work in your life? What significant people or important events led up to your salvation? In what ways would you describe your life since coming to know Christ? Use the space on the following page to make your own chart, drawing a personal itinerary of His story in your life.

Chart of God's Work in My Life

Chapter 4

FROM CREATION
TO A NATION

Survey of Genesis through Deuteronomy

At last, we're ready to begin! Our mental motors are warmed up, our minds are packed, and it's time to hit the road for a fascinating tour of God's grand Route 66.

Yessir, we're going to see it all, starting with . . . with . . . hold it, STOP! Do you know exactly what places we're supposed to see today? No? But I thought *you* were looking at His map. Me? I was double-checking the doctrines of revelation, inspiration, and illumination.

All right, all right, let's not panic and start blaming one another. All I have to do is take a quick glance and . . . here it is, the first leg of our journey covers Genesis, Exodus, Leviticus, Numbers, and Deuteronomy. OK?

We're off again! Roll down the windows, let the cool breeze blow, and let's begin our epic journey through . . . uh, er . . . what was the name of this stretch of Scripture? Do you remember the name? I don't remember the name. Wait, pull over. We can't start without at least knowing the name of where we're going. Maybe it's on the back of this brochure, yes, here it is—the first five books of the Bible are frequently referred to as simply "the Law" (see Matt. 7:12; 22:36–40). This is interesting; they're also known by two other names. First, the "Pentateuch," from *pente*—"five," and *teuchos*, meaning "book"; and second, the "Torah," which is Hebrew for "Law" (see Exodus 16:4, where this same word is rendered "instruction").

All set then, here we go! It's the Law or bust. First stop, the panoramic view of primal history as recorded in Genesis by . . . by . . . oh, no. Don't tell me we forgot to bring along who wrote Genesis. We're never going to get started at this rate. Better stop and ask someone—oh, you remember? Moses, that's right! He wrote all five books we're about to visit.[1]

---

1. See Exodus 17:14; Joshua 8:30–32; Malachi 4:4; Mark 12:19, 26; and 2 Corinthians 3:15, where the first five books are associated with Moses.

So, *now* are we ready? You bet. Pentateuch, here we come!

A Closer Look into the Books

Our first stop is Genesis, a book that has been called "the seed plot of Scripture."

Genesis . . . the Book of Beginnings

"Beginnings" is precisely what the term *genesis* means and what occurs in the fertile pages of this first book of the Bible. For example, we find here the inception of

> the universe . . . time . . . this earth . . . the starry heavens . . . life . . . marriage and family . . . sin . . . redemption . . . civilization . . . languages . . . the races . . . divine judgment . . . government . . . and maybe a dozen other significant beginnings.

For fifty chapters, Moses narrates us through some of the most dramatic scenery of human history. Perhaps the simplest way to remember the founding events is to break this book down into two sections.

1. Chapters 1–11: *The earliest history of the human race.* In this first section are four great events.[2]

> Creation (chaps. 1–2)
> The Fall into sin (chap. 3)
> The Flood in the days of Noah (chaps. 6–9)
> The birth of the nations (chaps. 10–11)

2. Chapters 12–50: *The earliest history of the Hebrew race.* In this section are four great men.[3]

> Abraham—Father of the Jews (chaps. 12–25)
> Isaac—promised son (chaps. 25–26)
> Jacob—whose name was later changed to Israel (chaps. 27–36)
> Joseph—from pit to pinnacle, a man of character (chaps. 37–50)

2. This period covers thousands of years.

3. This period covers only about three hundred years.

Once Abraham was on the biblical scene, God covenanted to begin through him a distinctive race of people who would come to be known as Hebrews or Jews. Genesis 12:1–3 records the promise God made, which He ratified many times down through the centuries.

> Now the Lord said to Abram,
> "Go forth from your country,
> And from your relatives
> And from your father's house,
> To the land which I will show you;
> And I will make you a great nation,
> And I will bless you,
> And make your name great;
> And so you shall be a blessing;
> And I will bless those who bless you,
> And the one who curses you I will curse.
> And in you all the families of the earth shall
> be blessed."

From this time forward, God's focus is on His people whom He promised to bless and protect. Now note this carefully: simply put, the rest of the Old Testament is nothing more than a record of God's dealings with His people, the Jews, and His fulfillment of the promises stated in Genesis 12:1–3. One promise, in particular, was that "all the families of the earth shall be blessed" because of Abraham (v. 3). How? Because through him God preserved a messianic line through which the Redeemer, Christ Jesus, would be born.

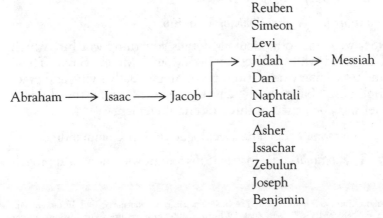

By the end of Genesis, the Hebrew people, now known as Israel, are settled and prospering in Egypt—thanks to Joseph, who had been promoted by Pharaoh to be his prime minister. With the last verse of the book, Moses then tells of Joseph's death, which brings us to the border of our next book.

Exodus . . . the Book of Deliverance

After Joseph's death, a new king arose in Egypt who feared the growing size and strength of the Jewish nation. So, he appointed taskmasters to afflict the people with hard labor (Exod. 1:8–11). After four hundred years of this bondage, the Lord raised up Moses to lead His people out of Egypt and to the Promised Land in Canaan.

As the title suggests, this second book covers that time when the Jews made their exodus out of Egypt. Geographically, the forty chapters of Exodus take us from the Hebrew ghetto in Egypt to Mount Sinai, where God gave His Law to Moses. Broken down into chapters, we could divide this particular portion of Israel's history into three sections.

- Chapters 1–12: The Hebrews are in Egypt

- Chapters 13–18: Israel goes from Egypt to Sinai

- Chapters 19–40: God's people are at Sinai

Once at Sinai, two significant events took place. First, the Israelites were given the moral law, the Ten Commandments (20:1–17); and second, they were given the blueprints and interior design for a portable place of worship—a tent church called the tabernacle (25:1–27:21; 35:4–38:31; 40:1–38).

Leviticus . . . the Book of Worship

Next we come to meticulous details governing worship, which Israel received while still encamped around Mount Sinai. These laws included "many regulations pertaining to daily living and practical holiness."[4] Basically, the Law God gave Moses for the children of Israel was comprised of three essential elements.

1. The *moral* code: The Decalogue or Ten Commandments

2. The *spiritual* code: Instructions for knowing how to approach

---

4. F. Duane Lindsey, "Leviticus," in *The Bible Knowledge Commentary*, Old Testament ed., ed. John F. Walvoord and Roy B. Zuck (Wheaton, Ill.: Scripture Press Publications, Victor Books, 1985), p. 164.

God and maintain fellowship with Him through blood sacrifices (key verse is Leviticus 17:11)

3. The *social* code: The practical side of life, covering everything from personal hygiene, soil conservation, and family life to maintaining their national distinctiveness

Numbers . . . the Book of Wanderings

Now, some people tend to wander off and get lost right about here because they fail to realize that, geographically, Numbers starts where Exodus stopped. So let's stay together as Israel moves out from Sinai and heads once again for the Promised Land (Num. 1:1–10:10).

Once the Israelites reached the edge of Canaan at a place named Kadesh, they sent in twelve spies to scout the land and its inhabitants. Ten returned convinced that it was hopeless to possess the land *even though God promised them it was theirs for the taking!* Because the people listened to the scouts and grumbled against God and Moses, all adults, aged twenty and older, were sentenced to die wandering in the wilderness.

It took forty years of aimless drifting before God's divine discipline was complete. The doubters were left in the dust of the desert as Israel's next generation emerged to claim Canaan for a second time. Thus, the history of Israel recorded in Numbers can be remembered using this simple outline:

- Chapters 1–14: The old generation

- Chapters 15–20: The wilderness wanderings

- Chapters 21–36: The new generation

The last chapters of Numbers record Israel's arrival at the plains of Moab, right on the southeast corner of the Promised Land. Once again Israel faced the choice of believing God or doubting His promise. This time there was no turning back. The Hebrews had learned an unforgettable lesson, but Moses drove it home to them in several sermons before they entered Canaan. These sermons are recorded at our next stop-off.

Deuteronomy . . . the Book of Transition

The title Deuteronomy means "second law," and in this book Moses reviews God's Law and warns the people against disobeying His words. It is a momentous time of transition for Israel. They're about to exchange their nomadic ways to become wealthy home owners in a rich land. Knowing that prosperity brings its own subtle temptations, Moses charges the people again and again to not forget the cost of disobedience and to love and obey the Lord without doubt or failure. He does this beginning in chapters 1–11 by looking backward to review and reflect on Israel's history from Mount Sinai to the present at Moab. Then, in chapters 12–34, he looks forward, reminding and reassuring them of God's laws and blessing on their obedience.[5]

Sadly, this first leg of our journey ends with the death of that great deliverer, leader, lawgiver, and guide—Moses. Let's pull aside in Deuteronomy 34 and pay our last respects to the prophet who paved the way for us through the first five books of the Bible.

> Now Moses went up from the plains of Moab to Mount Nebo, to the top of Pisgah, which is opposite Jericho. And the Lord showed him all the land, Gilead as far as Dan, and all Naphtali and the land of Ephraim and Manasseh, and all the land of Judah as far as the western sea, and the Negev and the plain in the valley of Jericho, the city of palm trees, as far as Zoar. Then the Lord said to him, "This is the land which I swore to Abraham, Isaac, and Jacob, saying, 'I will give it to your descendants'; I have let you see it with your eyes, but you shall not go over there." So Moses the servant of the Lord died there in the land of Moab, according to the word of the Lord. And He buried him in the valley in the land of Moab, opposite Beth-peor; but no man knows his burial place to this day. Although Moses was one hundred and twenty years old when he died, his eye was not dim, nor his vigor abated. So the sons of Israel wept for Moses in the plains of Moab thirty days; then the days of weeping and mourning for Moses came to an end. (vv. 1–8)

5. For a more detailed outline of Moses' speeches, see *The Bible Knowledge Commentary*, pp. 260–61.

Concluding Thought

Just about everyone who has gone on a long road trip returns with a whole trunkful of souvenirs. Everything from spoons to postcards to pictures. A memory we'd like for you to treasure from our travels today is a parallel between the books we've toured and an outline of the Christian's experience in God's family.

As in Genesis, we all had our *beginning*. We came to God by faith in His Son, Jesus Christ. As in Exodus, we were *delivered*, led out from our bondage to sin to become God's people. As in Leviticus, we were then introduced to real *worship*, to the pursuit of personal holiness out of obedience to a holy God. As in Numbers, we've all experienced *wanderings* and periods of disobedience when God had to discipline us. And as in Deuteronomy, we need *reviews* and *reminders* of God's laws and His faithfulness to strengthen our faith.

 Living Insights STUDY ONE

It's important not only that we follow God's Route 66 but that we remember it. Take a moment to review the itinerary from our chapter by filling in the blanks. Also, we'll leave you some space following each book of the Bible to write a brief summary of the significant people and events pertaining to that section.

Genesis . . . the Book of _____

    Chapters 1–11: The history of the _____

    Chapters 12–50: The history of the _____

_____

_____

_____

———◆———

Exodus . . . the Book of _____

    Chapters 1–12: In _____

    Chapters 13–18: From _____ to _____

Chapters 19–40: At _____

_____

_____

_____

———◆———

Leviticus . . . the Book of _____

    God's Law: 1. The _____ code

             2. The _____ code

             3. The _____ code

_____

_____

_____

———◆———

Numbers . . . the Book of _____

    Chapters 1–14: The _____ generation

    Chapters 15–20: The _____ _____

    Chapters 21–36: The _____ generation

_____

_____

_____

———◆———

Deuteronomy . . . the Book of _____

    Chapters 1–11: Looking _____

    Chapters 12–34: Looking _____

_____

_____

_____

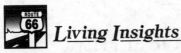 *Living Insights*

If you were to describe your own Christian experience right now, which of the five books from our study would you choose?

Genesis: Is this a time of new beginnings, new challenges for you?

Exodus: Have you recently escaped a difficult situation, relationship, or addiction that held you in bondage?

Leviticus: Are you enjoying a unique time of intimacy with God through worship?

Numbers: Does life feel like a wilderness right now, barren and lonely?

Deuteronomy: Has God reminded or warned you recently of some key spiritual truth He wants you to remember?

Use the following space to name the book that best describes you and explain why.

_____

_____

_____

_____

_____

_____

Chapter 5

THE RISE OF THE HEBREW NATION

Survey of Joshua through 2 Samuel

As we get ready to put our minds in gear and take off down God's Route 66 again, let's warm up our engines with a brief overview of today's itinerary.

A Survey Chart of Five Historical Books

Book/Chapters	Main Characters	Major Theme
Joshua (24)	Joshua	Invasion, conquest, and distribution of the land of Canaan.
Judges (21)	Thirteen leaders who served as judges among the Jews.	Repeated cycles of disobedience, bondage, deliverance, and peace (a depressing book).
Ruth (4)	Ruth and Boaz	Domestic scene during the period of the judges.
1 Samuel (31)	Samuel, Saul, and David	Beginning of the Hebrew monarchy.
2 Samuel (24)	David	Establishment, growth, and development of the united kingdom.

These five historical books trace the Hebrews' transformation from a scruffy tribe of nomads to a powerful, united nation. In the midst of this transformation, Israel's form of government also changed from a theocracy, with God as the ruler, to a monarchy, where various men will assume the role of king.

We have a lot of ground to cover, don't we! So let's begin right away with the story of Moses' successor in the book of Joshua.

Five Books That Continue the Story

In our last lesson, we left off with Moses' death on Mount Nebo just as Israel's new generation was about to enter Canaan. Now it is Joshua's turn to lead; now it is time for fighting, for military strategy, for overcoming the Canaanites, and settling down in a new land.

Joshua . . . a Book of Conquest

Now it came about after the death of Moses the servant of the Lord that the Lord spoke to Joshua the son of Nun, Moses' servant, saying, "Moses My servant is dead; now therefore arise, cross this Jordan, you and all this people, to the land which I am giving to them, to the sons of Israel. Every place on which the sole of your foot treads, I have given it to you, just as I spoke to Moses. From the wilderness and this Lebanon, even as far as the great river, the river Euphrates, all the land of the Hittites, and as far as the Great Sea toward the setting of the sun, will be your territory. No man will be able to stand before you all the days of your life. Just as I have been with Moses, I will be with you; I will not fail you or forsake you. Be strong and courageous, for you shall give this people possession of the land which I swore to their fathers to give them." (Josh. 1:1–6)

And Joshua was strong and courageous in leading the conquest of Canaan, as the following outline of his book shows.

I. Chapters 1–5: Invasion of the land

II. Chapters 6–12: Subjection of the land
   A. Central campaign (chaps. 6–9)
   B. Southern campaign (chap. 10)
   C. Northern campaign (chap. 11; key verse is 11:23)

III. Chapters 13–22: Distribution of the land

IV. Chapters 23–24: Joshua commissions the people

Even though Joshua's campaign into Canaan was overwhelmingly successful, all of Israel's enemies were not killed or driven out. Many pagans remained deeply entrenched in various pockets of the Promised Land. So each Hebrew tribe was commissioned to carry on the task of expelling their adversaries in whichever part of the country they settled. To that commission Joshua added this warning:

"Be very firm, then, to keep and do all that is written

41

in the book of the law of Moses, so that you may not turn aside from it to the right hand or to the left, in order that you may not associate with these nations, these which remain among you, or mention the name of their gods, or make anyone swear by them, or serve them, or bow down to them. But you are to cling to the Lord your God, as you have done to this day. . . . Take diligent heed to yourselves to love the Lord your God. For if you ever go back and cling to the rest of these nations, these which remain among you, and intermarry with them, so that you associate with them and they with you, know with certainty that the Lord your God will not continue to drive these nations out from before you; but they shall be a snare and a trap to you, and a whip on your sides and thorns in your eyes, until you perish from off this good land which the Lord your God has given you." (23:6–8, 11–13)

Obey and prosper, disobey and suffer—the choice was Israel's. And the Hebrews made a bad one. Several bad ones.

Judges . . . a Book of Compromise

The first verse of this book is a telling one.

Now it came about after the death of Joshua that the sons of Israel inquired of the Lord, saying, "Who shall go up first for us against the Canaanites, to fight against them?" (Judg. 1:1)

Without a strong leader like Joshua to anchor the people's faith in the Lord and lead them in battle, Israel drifted in both spiritual and military commitments. The people failed to finish the task of driving their enemies completely out of Canaan. Instead of stunning victories, they settled for chummy compromises. "Everyone did what was right in his own eyes" (21:25), and the consequences were disastrous.

Look closely at the steps that led to their downfall:

1. They failed to drive out the heathens (1:28).

2. They became idolatrous, like the heathens (see 2:10–12).

3. They intermarried with the heathens (3:6–7).

The Israelites lost their distinctiveness as a holy people, and that always resulted in one thing—bondage, God's promised discipline. And this didn't happen just once, mind you, but again and again in a cycle of misery that can be summed up in five words: *liberation* . . . which led to *relaxation* . . . which led to *deterioration* . . . which led to *subjugation* . . . which led to *petition* . . . which led, by God's grace, back to *liberation*.

Each time the Israelites humbled themselves before God, He sent them a deliverer known as a "judge" to free them from their bondage. What do we know about these remarkable people? First, unlike kings, these individuals were not chosen on the basis of royal birth. Second, they were local tribal heroes more often than national ones. Third, for the most part, they were military leaders. And fourth, they were typically recognized as leaders after they had freed part of the nation from bondage. Rather than being chosen or appointed as judge, they earned the title, much like a general in the military.

Altogether, thirteen of these heroes are etched in the history of Judges, and we should at least honor them by acknowledging their names.

1. Othniel (3:8–11)
2. Ehud (3:12–30)
3. Shamgar (3:31)
4. Deborah (4:4–5:31)
5. Barak (4:6–5:31)
6. Gideon (6:11–8:32)
7. Tola (10:1–2)
8. Jair (10:3–5)
9. Jephthah (11:1–12:7)
10. Ibzan (12:8–10)
11. Elon (12:11–12)
12. Abdon (12:13–15)
13. Samson (13:1–16:31)[1]

The book of Judges is a dismal account of some of Israel's darkest days. It begins with disobedience and ends in horror and disgrace. Yet in the midst of this ugly stretch of history, God has preserved an oasis in our next book.

1. Even though Eli and Samuel are judges, they are not listed here because they do not appear on the pages of Scripture until the book of 1 Samuel. Just in case all these strange names sound dull and boring to you, let us whet your appetite for the interesting history you'll uncover in Judges by suggesting you preview either 3:15–25 or 4:16–22.

Ruth . . . a Book of Love

This is the moving story of a young Moabitess named Ruth who lived, most likely, during the early days of the judges. Her story assures us that not every home was wicked during that period of Israel's history. Love, godliness, and grace mark the domestic scene tucked in the folds of the following outline.

Ruth's choice . . . . Chapter 1

Ruth's occupation. . . . . Chapter 2

Ruth's claim . . . . Chapter 3

Ruth's reward . . . . Chapter 4

Commentator John W. Reed provides a brief synopsis of this book's high points.

> The Book of Ruth is named for a Moabitess who had married a Hebrew man living in Moab. After the death of her husband, Ruth migrated with Naomi, her widowed Hebrew mother-in-law, to Bethlehem in Israel. There God providentially provided for her and led her to marry Boaz, a prosperous Hebrew farmer. Ruth became the great-grandmother of King David. She is listed in the genealogy of Christ in Matthew 1:5.[2]

The book of Ruth begins with loss and ends with gain. It begins with sorrow and ends with joy. It begins with death and ends, not only with life, but with a son whose descendants will ultimately give birth to "the way, and the truth, and the life"—Jesus.

1 and 2 Samuel . . . Two Books of Tragedy, Triumphs, and Trials

The first book of Samuel covers the transitional period when Israel's government shifted from theocracy to monarchy. Why would the Hebrews make such an unwise trade? Let's turn to 1 Samuel 8 for some answers.

---

2. John W. Reed, "Ruth," in *The Bible Knowledge Commentary*, Old Testament ed., ed. John F. Walvoord and Roy B. Zuck (Wheaton, Ill.: Scripture Press Publications, Victor Books, 1985), p. 415.

And it came about when Samuel was old that he appointed his sons judges over Israel. . . . His sons, however, did not walk in his ways, but turned aside after dishonest gain and took bribes and perverted justice.

Then all the elders of Israel gathered together and came to Samuel at Ramah; and they said to him, "Behold, you have grown old, and your sons do not walk in your ways. Now appoint a king for us to judge us like all the nations." (vv. 1, 3–5)

The people of Israel gave Samuel three reasons for wanting a king (v. 5):

1. Samuel was too old to continue.

2. Samuel's sons were unfit to replace him.

3. They wanted to be like all the other nations.

Following Samuel (chaps. 1–8), the next significant person to appear is Saul, Israel's first king (chaps. 9–15). For the first time in their history, the Jews became a united kingdom under one human monarch. And though Saul was humble in the beginning, he became proud, rash, stubborn, and disobedient to the Lord.

The third significant person to take center stage in 1 Samuel is Israel's second king, David (chaps. 16–31). He was insanely envied by his predecessor, Saul, but never retaliated for all the king's mistreatment of him. And even though he was anointed as king by Samuel, David graciously waited until after Saul's death before assuming the throne.

Five significant chapters to remember from this book are:

• Chapter 8: Why do you want a king?

• Chapter 16: David is anointed.

• Chapter 17: David fights Goliath.

• Chapter 28: Saul makes a desperate visit to the witch of En-dor.

• Chapter 31: Saul commits suicide.

Where Saul failed miserably as Israel's first king, David succeeded beyond anyone's wildest imaginations, as we shall see in our next and final stop, 2 Samuel.

In the early part of his reign, recorded in chapters 1–11, David never knew military defeat or domestic conflict. He rose to an unparalleled pinnacle of power, godliness, and prosperity. Here is just a scant list of some of his achievements:

1. He unified and strengthened the nation.

2. He obtained a royal capital.

3. He developed Israel into a military power.

4. He subdued all her enemies.

5. He extended her boundaries from approximately 6,000 to 60,000 square miles.

6. He created national pride.

7. He brought dignity and respect to the nation's throne.

8. He extended trade to other nations.

9. He provided Israel with her greatest period of prosperity in her long history.

Yet all this he put at risk with a forbidden affair. For from the moment he sinned with Bathsheba and then tried to cover it up, trouble and pain haunted the man to his grave.

So if you were to draw a diagram of 2 Samuel, it would resemble a rooftop. Everything leading up to chapter 11 is great and successful, and everything from chapter 11 to the end of the book slopes down with sadness and disappointment.

Another way of looking at this stretch of biblical history is to outline it by chapters.

David's successes and triumphs . . . . Chapters 1–10

David's failure and troubles . . . . Chapters 11–22

David's last days . . . . Chapters 23–24

Despite his failure and the ensuing consequences, though, David's was still the reign referred to again and again in Scripture as the model for other kings to follow. Also, David is referred to more often in the New Testament than any other Old Testament individual.

Concluding Thought

We've covered many, many miles of Israel's history along this section of God's Route 66. Looking back in our rearview mirrors, we can still remember seeing the Hebrews in battle and bondage, conquering and compromising, strong and weak. Through it all, we can also see that God never abandoned His people or broke the promise He had made with Abraham. The Lord brought the Jews into their land, made their nation great, and blessed them abundantly. Why? G-r-a-c-e! The same undeserved favor He extends to all of us. For we can all look in the rearview mirrors of our lives and note similar patterns of advance and retreat, victory and defeat. Nevertheless, He continues to love us as He did them. He knows us the best and loves us the most, and nothing any of us does as His children can ever separate us from His love.

> Who shall separate us from the love of Christ? Shall tribulation, or distress, or persecution, or famine, or nakedness, or peril, or sword? . . . For I am convinced that neither death, nor life, nor angels, nor principalities, nor things present, nor things to come, nor powers, nor height, nor depth, nor any other created thing, shall be able to separate us from the love of God, which is in Christ Jesus our Lord. (Rom. 8:35, 38–39)

 Living Insights

The road ahead is not always clear. Some days the fog of uncertainty blocks our vision. Some days the driving rain of bitter tears blinds us. Some days adversity blackens everything, leaving us to grope and stumble in a dark night of the soul. And then there are those beautiful rain-rinsed, wind-spun, sun-drenched days when the road before us suddenly seems magnified as if to say, "Here, look, rejoice! God is good, there is hope!" We can see again—and it feels good.

Looking ahead, however, is not all that lightens our hearts. It's also catching a breathtaking glimpse in our rearview mirrors of how God's grace guided us through the difficult times when we felt blinded and alone. And we must carefully record those glimpses of

His grace in our hearts. For when the road ahead becomes obscured again, and it will, our best comfort is to retrace His faithfulness in the past.

How many years of bondage and despair would have been avoided if the people of Israel had only remembered God's faithfulness each time they faced a seeming roadblock? Think of the detours and dead ends they experienced because they constantly forgot and complained instead of remembering and trusting.

None of us know what road conditions we will face tomorrow. What we can know is that God will not forsake us, just as He did not forsake the children of Israel. Take a moment to look in the rearview mirror of your own life and record the glimpses of His grace that you see.

_____

_____

_____

_____

_____

The next time the road ahead is not clear, focus on what is— God's faithfulness to you.

> Let your character be free from the love of money,
> being content with what you have; for He Himself
> has said, "I will never desert you, nor will I ever
> forsake you," so that we confidently say,
>   "The Lord is my helper, I will not be afraid.
>   What shall man do to me?" (Heb. 13:5–6)

 Living Insights STUDY TWO

OK, all right, just give me a second. Let's see . . . uh, Moses invaded Canaan and, no . . . Joshua conquered Mount Nebo and then divided the Promised Land to thirteen judges who compromised with the pagans and then Ruth joined up with Othneilli and Ishbomb and stopped the cycle of, of, er I think it was deterioration, libation, and incarceration. Then the children of Israel wanted a king so they chose Samuel who was humble at first and later committed suicide. David came next and when he saw Bathsheba, he fell off the roof.

How's that? Not so good, huh? Do you think you could help me out here? Use the space provided to reconstruct the highlights of the road just covered in our lesson—without peeking in the rearview mirror at the lesson either, of course! Let's see what you really remember.

_____

_____

_____

_____

_____

_____

_____

_____

Chapter 6

THE DECLINE AND FALL
OF THE HEBREW NATION

Survey of 1 Kings through 2 Chronicles

Are we there yet?

Well, not quite. We've come a long way, though. Speeding along God's Route 66, we've traveled through the lives of the patriarchs, across the hardships of the wilderness, and into the Promised Land and the rise of the Hebrew nation. It's been an eventful trip, but we still have a way to go . . . and the roughest stretch of road is just ahead.

As we enter the books of Kings and Chronicles, potholes of idolatry and pride will crater the highway. Cracks of immorality will snake across the interstate. Eventually, the road will disintegrate into a jigsaw puzzle of buckling asphalt. Better fasten your seat belts for a rugged ride!

What caused this national destruction? A slow and silent force called erosion. Roads—or nations or marriages or businesses—don't crumble suddenly; it takes years of steady, thoughtless decay. And most of the time no one notices until everything starts falling apart, but then it is too late.

The collapse of the Roman Empire illustrates this process. Edward Gibbon, in his *Decline and Fall of the Roman Empire*, located five eroding rivers that washed out Rome's foundation:

1. An undermining of the dignity and sanctity of the home, which is the basis for human society.

2. Higher and higher taxes, and spending public money for free bread and circuses for the populace.

3. A mad craze for pleasure, with pastimes becoming every year more exciting, brutal, and immoral.

4. Building great armaments, although the real enemy was within—the decay of individual responsibility.

5. Decay of religion—faith fading into mere

50

form, losing touch with life and losing power to guide the people.[1]

It wasn't military might that really conquered the empire; Rome fell from the inside out.

Israel followed a similar course of internal collapse. The period of Jewish history we'll journey through in this chapter is tragic . . . and, we might add, rather complicated. To get our bearings, let's spread out a historical map and trace the route that leads us through the decline and fall of the Hebrew nation.

How It All Fits Together

SURVEY CHART OF THE UNITED AND DIVIDED KINGDOMS

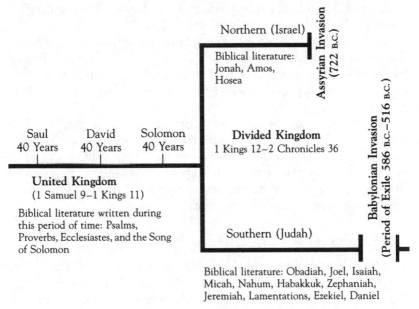

Saul's forty-year reign over Israel's twelve tribes marked the beginning of the united kingdom period (see 1 Sam. 9–31). When Saul died, the crown passed to David, who also reigned forty years

---

1. Edward Gibbon, as quoted by Lloyd Cory, comp., in *Quotable Quotations* (Wheaton, Ill.: Scripture Press Publications, Victor Books, 1985), pp. 179–80.

(see 2 Sam. 1–24). Then he handed the scepter to his son Solomon, who ruled forty more years (see 1 Kings 1–11).

During the united kingdom period, David and Solomon penned their most exquisite spiritual poetry, including portions of Psalms and Proverbs, the book of Ecclesiastes, and the Song of Solomon. Under their influence, the scattered seeds of the twelve tribes grew into a single, luxuriant vine, and the world marveled at the flourishing little country with its burgeoning treasury and magnificent temple.[2]

However, when Solomon's son, Rehoboam, came to power, he foolishly tried governing the people with an iron grip. In 931 B.C., the northern ten tribes shook free of his tyranny, seceding to form their own nation and crown their own king—the wicked Jeroboam. Thus the beautiful vine split apart and the divided kingdom period began.

For 209 years, the rebel flag waved over the northern kingdom. Twenty kings paraded across its landscape, and all of them followed Jeroboam's sinful example. Finally, in 722 B.C., the Assyrian army wielded its sword, and the northern kingdom collapsed in the sinkhole of its own sin.

Meanwhile, the southern kingdom clung to the map for 136 more years. As in the north, twenty kings mounted the throne. Most of them were bad, but about eight of them were godly, rejuvenating memories of David's golden years. These good kings slowed the spiritual erosion, but they could not stop it; and in 586 B.C., the Babylonians destroyed Jerusalem.[3]

Three Keys That Help Unlock the Mystery

Northern kingdom, southern kingdom . . . good kings, bad kings . . . names like Amaziah and Ahaziah . . . Joram and Jehoram . . . Elijah and Elisha. It's downright baffling! To unlock some of the mystery surrounding this period of Jewish history, here are three keys to slip into your mental pocket.

2. The complete history of the united kingdom period is found in 1 Samuel 9 through 1 Kings 11.

3. The complete history of the divided kingdom period is found in 1 Kings 12 through 2 Kings 25. First and 2 Chronicles survey the united kingdom as well as the divided kingdom periods. The Chronicles begin with nine chapters of genealogies, then pick up the story with the death of Saul in 1 Chronicles 10, and finish with the destruction of Jerusalem and Cyrus' decree to rebuild the temple in 2 Chronicles 36.

First, *understand that a civil war has occurred.* Consequently, the writers of Kings and Chronicles must trace the history of two nations at the same time. Sometimes the authors highlight the southern kingdom in one chapter, then switch to the northern kingdom in the next. While you read the accounts, try to determine which side of the border the author is talking about, the northern or the southern.

To do that requires a second key: *remember the titles given to the kingdoms.* Let's look at a few of the names the writers use.

The Northern Kingdom	The Southern Kingdom
Israel	Judah
Ephraim	Jerusalem
Samaria	

Finally, *keep on hand a list of the kings and their reigns.* A Bible dictionary or a good chart of this period will help you keep straight the reigns of the kings. The chart we have provided at the end of this chapter shows where the many prophets and their ministries to specific nations and kings fit in.

And Now . . . a General Overview of this Era

Now, with our map open on the seat beside us, let's resume our trip, looking out for signs of spiritual erosion.

The United Kingdom

The stretch of highway before us first crosses through the united kingdom period. Having already passed by the reigns of Saul and David in the last chapter, let's continue through Solomon's reign— which begins with some very impressive scenery.

> Now God gave Solomon wisdom and very great discernment and breadth of mind, like the sand that is on the seashore. And Solomon's wisdom surpassed the wisdom of all the sons of the east and all the wisdom of Egypt. . . . He also spoke 3,000 proverbs, and his songs were 1,005. And he spoke of trees, from the cedar that is in Lebanon even to the hyssop that grows on the wall; he spoke also of animals and birds and creeping things and fish. And men came from all peoples to hear the wisdom of Solomon, from all the kings of the earth who had heard of his wisdom. (1 Kings 4:29–30, 32–34)

Even the famous queen of Sheba heard about Solomon's wisdom and wealth. Wanting to see him for herself and "test him with difficult questions," she led a great caravan of camels bearing gold and jewels and precious spices up the slopes to Jerusalem (10:1–2). When Solomon answered her questions, and when she saw "the house that he had built,

> the food of his table, the seating of his servants, the attendance of his waiters and their attire, his cup-bearers, and his stairway by which he went up to the house of the Lord, there was no more spirit in her. (vv. 4b–5)

Putting it in today's terms, she was blown away! Solomon's glittering palace was like an ancient Fort Knox.

> Now the weight of gold which came in to Solomon in one year was 666 talents of gold, besides that from the traders and the wares of the merchants and all the kings of the Arabs and the governors of the country. . . . Moreover, the king made a great throne of ivory and overlaid it with refined gold. . . . And all King Solomon's drinking vessels were of gold, and all the vessels of the house of the forest of Lebanon were of pure gold. None was of silver; it was not considered valuable in the days of Solomon. . . .
> So King Solomon became greater than all the kings of the earth in riches and in wisdom. (vv. 14–15, 18, 21, 23)

Yet no amount of gold could overlay the sin eroding Solomon's soul. The first breach appeared in his uncontrolled affections.

> Now King Solomon loved many foreign women along with the daughter of Pharaoh: Moabite, Ammonite, Edomite, Sidonian, and Hittite women, from the nations concerning which the Lord had said to the sons of Israel, "You shall not associate with them, neither shall they associate with you, for they will surely turn your heart away after their gods." Solomon held fast to these in love. And he had seven hundred wives, princesses, and three hundred concubines, and his wives turned his heart

away. For it came about when Solomon was old, his wives turned his heart away after other gods; and his heart was not wholly devoted to the Lord his God, as the heart of David his father had been. (11:1–4)

Tragically, when it came to matters of the heart, wise Solomon acted the fool. Wanting to please his wives more than the Lord, he set up idols in Jerusalem and joined in the worship (vv. 5–8). Eventually, what began as a crack within the king's heart for the Lord led to a yawning rift within the nation when the kingdom divided into north and south. Overall, four factors contributed to the split of the kingdom:

• *spiritual decline*, due to the influx of idolatry

• *economic burden*, from Solomon and his son overworking and overtaxing the people (12:3–14)

• *political competition with Jeroboam*, whom the people of Israel chose to be their king (vv. 1–2, 20)

• *moral and personal failures in Solomon's family*, because they broke God's covenant

The Divided Kingdom

Bump. Jar. Clatter. Jolt. Got your seat belt on? The road through the history of the northern kingdom, Israel, gets rougher and rougher. Finally, everything crumbles under the chariot wheels of the mighty Assyrian army (see 2 Kings 17:22–24).

The southern kingdom, Judah, miraculously resisted the Assyrian invasion, thanks to the spiritual leadership of Hezekiah (see 2 Chron. 32:9–23). But subsequent generations turned away from God, so "the wrath of the Lord arose against His people,

until there was no remedy. Therefore He brought up against them the king of the Chaldeans who slew their young men with the sword in the house of their sanctuary, and had no compassion on young man or virgin, old man or infirm; He gave them all into his hand. (36:16b–17)

The weeping prophet, Jeremiah, described the horror of this holocaust in the book bearing his own name (see Jer. 52:1–34). Survivors were taken to Babylon as exiles for seventy years—the number of years the nation ignored God's Sabbath requirements for the land (2 Chron. 36:20–21; see also Lev. 25:4, 11; 26:34–35).

Exile

While in exile, the people lingered over each sunset, yearning to follow the sun to their homeland in the west. During this period, Jeremiah wrote the book of Lamentations.[4] From Babylon, Ezekiel and Daniel were written, as well as a few of the psalms—such as the mournful Psalm 137:

> By the rivers of Babylon,
> There we sat down and wept,
> When we remembered Zion.
> Upon the willows in the midst of it
> We hung our harps.
> For there our captors demanded of us songs,
> And our tormentors mirth, saying,
> "Sing us one of the songs of Zion."
> How can we sing the Lord's song
> In a foreign land? (vv. 1–4)

We leave the Jews in their tears, bearing the full weight of their sorrow. But God does not abandon them. He hears their cries and is behind the scenes, protecting His people during their exile. Eventually, the Persian king, Cyrus, allows the Jews to return to Palestine (see 2 Chron. 36:22–23), and the historical books of Ezra and Nehemiah describe their triumphant rebuilding of the temple and the city walls in Jerusalem.

Two Lasting Lessons to Be Learned

For now, as we drive slowly and somberly through the rubble of the Hebrew nation, we see two principles rising from the dust. First, *enjoying the blessings of obedience is a rewarding but responsible way of life*. Gardeners, for example, must be responsible throughout the year to prepare the soil, sow the seeds, and nurture the young plants if they expect to enjoy the spring flowers. In the same way, we must daily pursue an obedient lifestyle in order to enjoy the blessings of obedience.

4. Jeremiah wrote Lamentations from the rubble that was Jerusalem. Unlike the other prophets, he didn't go to Babylon but later went with a remnant which fled to Egypt.

This brings us to a sobering second principle: *enduring the consequences of sin is a painful but permanent method of instruction.* Anyone who has endured divine discipline and suffered the consequences of wandering away from God has that lesson painfully and permanently etched in his or her heart. Also there, though, and held ever so sensitively and delicately, is the restorative touch of God's gracious forgiveness and His gift of "a future and a hope" (Jer. 29:11).

The decline and fall of the Hebrew nation is a warning to all who pass by—a reminder of the tragic results of erosion of the heart. So keep your heart pure and devoted to the Lord. And if you see sinkholes or crumbling pavement in the path you're on, don't despair. Turn and take the high, hopeful road of repentance.

 Living Insights   STUDY ONE

Are there any hairline cracks developing in your devotion to Christ? Only you and the Lord really know what is going on beneath the surface of your life. Invite Him right now for an inspection tour of your heart. Let Him reveal to you any signs of spiritual erosion that you may be overlooking. Take a moment to pray David's prayer as your own:

> Search me, O God, and know my heart;
> Try me and know my anxious thoughts;
> And see if there be any hurtful way in me,
> And lead me in the everlasting way.
> (Ps. 139:23–24)

We'll leave you some space to record what the Lord may reveal. As your pen flows across the page, let it spill out your confession to God.

_____

_____

_____

Now ask for Christ's forgiveness; allow it to repair the cracks and build a solid foundation of obedience in your life.

How blessed is he whose transgression is forgiven,

Whose sin is covered!
How blessed is the man to whom the Lord does not
impute iniquity,
And in whose spirit there is no deceit! (Ps. 32:1–2)

 Living Insights

Confession is such a profoundly simple way to protect ourselves against the effects of spiritual erosion—even a child can do it. Yet Solomon didn't. Why do you think this man who was so wise refused to face the destructive sin in his heart? You may want to reread the account of his downfall in 1 Kings 11:1–8.

_____

_____

_____

_____

Jesus said, "Where your treasure is, there will your heart be also" (Matt. 6:21). Sadly, Solomon's great treasures and passions stole his heart away from the Lord. If that can happen to the wisest, richest, most powerful man on earth, it can happen to us. Is there anything or any person in your life that is robbing your devotion to the Lord? If so, what do you need to do to restore your first love to Christ?

_____

_____

_____

_____

_____

As the years go by, remember Solomon. Never outgrow your need for confession, no matter how old or wise or powerful you become. And always view Christ as your richest treasure.

🔨 Digging Deeper

The return of the exiled Jews to Palestine is a fascinating story. The Lord had promised them, through the prophet Jeremiah:

> "When seventy years have been completed for Babylon, I will visit you and fulfill My good word to you, to bring you back to this place. For I know the plans that I have for you," declares the Lord, "plans for welfare and not for calamity to give you a future and a hope." (Jer. 29:10–11)

For years, they waited in exile for their Shepherd to lead them home. Finally,

> the Lord stirred up the spirit of Cyrus king of Persia, so that he sent a proclamation throughout his kingdom, and also put it in writing, saying, "Thus says Cyrus king of Persia, 'The Lord, the God of heaven, has given me all the kingdoms of the earth, and He has appointed me to build Him a house in Jerusalem, which is in Judah. Whoever there is among you of all His people, may the Lord his God be with him, and let him go up!'" (2 Chron. 36:22b–23)

And "go up" they did! Zerubbabel led the first group of returning Jews, and right away, they started rebuilding the temple. After the foundation was laid, though, their torrent of enthusiasm dried to a trickle when local inhabitants opposed them, and an edict from King Artaxerxes stopped them "by force of arms" (Ezra 4:23). For sixteen years, the project lay undone, until Haggai and Zechariah rallied them to finish construction. Finally, in 516 B.C., the temple stood once more—seventy years after its destruction.[5]

Later, around 458 B.C., Ezra led the second band of Jews to Palestine. He passionately preached spiritual commitment to the new generation of Jews, who had already begun showing signs of internal erosion just like their forefathers—compromising the Law

---

5. There are two ways to calculate the fulfillment of Jeremiah's prophecy that Judah would be in exile for seventy years. One view figures it from the destruction of the temple in 586 B.C. to its completion in 516 B.C. Another view figures it from Nebuchadnezzar's first deportation of Jews, such as Daniel, in 605 B.C. to the beginning of the temple's reconstruction in 536 B.C.

and marrying foreign women. Remember Solomon's fall?

Ezra's spiritual reforms paved the way for Nehemiah, who led a third group of Jews from Babylon around 445 b.c. Under his leadership, the people rebuilt the walls of the city in record-setting time: fifty-two days (Neh. 6:15).

The flock of Israel was home, and yet . . . In the years that followed, they would wander away from the fold and wolfish leaders would steal away their hearts. Eventually, the Good Shepherd Himself would come and provide them and us entrance to a lasting spiritual home in heaven. But that's another story . . . we have four centuries and three more chapters of road to travel before then!

Kings of Judah and Israel and the Preexilic Prophets

JUDAH

Kings	Dates	Years
Rehoboam	931–913	17
Abijah	913–911	3
Asa	911–870	41
Coregency with Jehoshaphat	873–870	(3)
Jehoshaphat	873–848	25
Coregency with Jehoram	853–848	(5)
Jehoram	848–841	8
Ahaziah OBADIAH	841	1
Queen Athaliah	841–835	6
Joash JOEL	835–796	40
Amaziah	796–767	29
Azariah's vice-regency under Amaziah	790–767	(23)
Azariah (Uzziah)	790–739	52
Coregency with Jotham	750–739	(11)
Jotham	750–735	16
Ahaz's vice-regency under Jotham	744–735	(9)
Coregency of Jotham with Ahaz	735–732	4
Ahaz	732–715	16
Hezekiah's vice-regency under Ahaz	729–715	(14)
Hezekiah	715–686	29
Manasseh's vice-regency under Hezekiah	697–686	(11)
Manasseh	697–642	55
Amon NAHUM	642–640	2
Josiah ZEPHANIAH	640–609	31
Johoahaz	609	1/4
Jehoiakim HABAKKUK	609–598	11
Jehoiachin	598–597	1/4
Zedekiah	597–586	11

(Prophets marked along left margin: MICAH, ISAIAH, JEREMIAH)

ISRAEL

Kings	Dates	Years
Jeroboam I	931–910	22
Nadab	910–909	2
Baasha	909–886	24
Elah	886–885	2
Zimri	885	7 days
Tibni	885–880	6
Overlapping reign with Omri	885–880	(6)
Omri	885–874	12
Ahab	874–853	22
Ahaziah	853–852	2
Jehoram (Joram)	852–841	12
Jehu	841–814	28
Jehoahaz	814–798	17
Jehoash (Joash)	798–782	16
Coregency with Jeroboam II	793–782	(11)
Jeroboam II JONAH	793–753	41
Zechariah AMOS	753–752	1/2
Shallum	752	1/12
Menahem	752–742	10
Overlapping reign with Pekah	752–742	(10)
Pekahiah	742–742	(2)
Overlapping reign with Pekah	742–740	(2)
Pekah	752–732	20
Hoshea	732–722	9

(Prophets marked along margin: ELIJAH, ELISHA, HOSEA)

Chart adapted from John F. Walvoord and Roy B. Zuck, eds., *The Bible Knowledge Commentary* (Wheaton, Ill.: Scripture Press Publications, Victor Books, 1985), p. 513.

Chapter 7

THE BOOKS OF POETRY
Survey of Job through Song of Solomon

Whew! After last chapter's jarring ride through Israel's decline and fall, it's time for a refreshing side trip. Let's exit the historical highway, roll back the top of our convertible—the *only* way to travel Route 66—breathe the clean mountain air, and enjoy the scenic beauty of God's Word. Which road shall we explore? Here's a section of Scripture with some spectacular vistas: the books of poetry—Job, Psalms, Proverbs, Ecclesiastes, and Song of Solomon.

It Is Helpful to Keep in Mind . . .

Since we'll be passing through a different literary style than that of the history books we've been through so far, a few facts about the poetical books will help prepare us for our trip. First, *each book has its own historical setting.* By understanding the author's world and his reasons for writing, we can gather important clues to unlocking the meaning of his poetry.

Job, for example, probably lived during the era of the patriarchs; he might have been a contemporary of Abraham. His book, then, is most likely the oldest of the Bible, written before Moses wrote Genesis. Psalms is a collection of songs written over many years, spanning the exodus from Egypt to the return of the exiles from Babylon. The bulk of the psalms, though, were written during the united kingdom era by King David himself. Ecclesiastes, Song of Solomon, and most of Proverbs were also penned before the kingdom split, during the reign of Solomon.

Second, *remember that Hebrew poetry does not rhyme.* Instead, the Hebrew writers used a poetic structure called parallelism—which is a good thing. It would be extremely difficult to translate rhyming Hebrew words into English and retain the poetic elegance. As it is, the poems can be translated into any language and the beauty remains.

The Hebrew authors relied on many forms of parallelism in their writing. For instance, they sometimes used *synonymous parallelism,* repeating an idea one line after the other:

He who sits in the heavens laughs,

62

The Lord scoffs at them.
(Ps. 2:4; see also 3:1; 5:1–3)

To contrast a thought, they also used *antithetical parallelism:*

For the Lord knows the way of the righteous,
But the way of the wicked will perish.
(Ps. 1:6; see also Prov. 16:1, 9, 25)

And they used *synthetic parallelism* to develop their thought through several lines that amplified or explained the first:

Bless the Lord, O my soul,
And forget none of His benefits;
Who pardons all your iniquities;
Who heals all your diseases;
Who redeems your life from the pit;
Who crowns you with lovingkindness and compassion;
Who satisfies your years with good things,
So that your youth is renewed like the eagle.
(Ps. 103:2–5; see also Prov. 2:1–5)[1]

Third, *poetry should be enjoyed rather than dissected and analyzed.* We miss the beauty of biblical poetry when we read it through a microscope, scrutinizing every noun and preposition to extract detailed doctrines. As works of art, like da Vinci's paintings or Mozart's symphonies, poetical books are meant to stir our souls and lift our hearts. The authors didn't craft them to be technical instruction manuals. They intended them to touch us on a more intimate level. According to commentator Ronald Allen:

Poetry is a special use of language. . . . Poetry is not designed basically to communicate information. One might wind up with a rather grotesque contraption were he to use a poem to build a barn. I would not wish to drive a car that was repaired by a mechanic on the basis of a poem. One might drown if he used a poem to learn how to swim. A good poem

1. According to Ronald Barclay Allen, there are two other types of parallelism: *climactic parallelism*, in which the second line takes some of the words from the first line and completes the idea (see Ps. 96:7); and *emblematic parallelism*, in which the second line explains the figure of speech in the first line (see Ps. 42:1). From *Praise: A Matter of Life and Breath* (Nashville, Tenn.: Thomas Nelson Publishers, 1980), pp. 52–53.

might, however, give me an experience of being in a barn, or driving, or swimming that could be intense and satisfying. Poetry is the language of experience.[2]

If we try to force the lyric loveliness of biblical poetry into the emotionless tones of theological treatises, we run the risk of misinterpreting the central truth of the poem or proverb. Most tragically, though, we miss an opportunity to share a common bond with the poets themselves, whose lives form some of the most striking scenery along our route through Scripture.

Brief but Probing Visits with Three Inspired Poets

Wending our way through the countryside, our first vista reveals the towering, weather-battered cliffs of the life of Job.

Job, a Businessman and Father Who Lost It All

Like the cracked and craggy layers of the cliffs, Job's life portrays a history of the calamitous storms he endured. The first two chapters of the book narrate the story of how he lost everything in one day: his servants . . . his business . . . his children. Later, he even lost his health when Satan afflicted him with excruciating boils covering his body. Yet, like the stalwart mountain face, his faith withstood the pressure to crumble, for "in all this Job did not sin with his lips" (Job 2:10b).

These first two chapters, then, are a practical narrative of this man's losing everything. Beginning in chapter 3, Job himself starts to speak in the expressive language of poetry. In this second section, chapters 3–37, "friends" counsel Job that he must have brought his suffering upon himself. "Sorry comforters are you all," he replies, contending that he is innocent (16:2b). A philosophical debate ensues, which offers the sufferer no relief; he needs the perspective only the Lord can offer. So in the poem's theological section, chapters 38–42, God answers Job out of the whirlwind, satisfying his inner turmoil. As the book closes, He restores Job's prosperity twofold.

This ancient poetry of Job touches those of us who must also endure the scouring winds of suffering. Job is our brother in pain; he knows how we feel when, on our journey through sorrow, we realize that no one really understands but God. He also reminds us

2. Allen, *Praise: A Matter of Life and Breath*, p. 44.

64

that although suffering is horrible, it teaches us our most permanent and priceless lessons about life. Job is a true poet.

David, a Shepherd-Musician Who Became a King

Our scenery changes from sheer cliffs to lush valleys as we come to the life of David—the shepherd, musician, and king. He's the songwriter of the Bible, composing the lyrics of nearly half the songs in the Hebrew hymnal, the book of Psalms. His psalms are particularly meaningful because they open a window into his soul during the best and worst times of his life.

Providing the historical backdrop to his poetry are the superscriptions that preface many of his psalms. For instance, the superscription for Psalm 18 tells us that David wrote this song

in the day that the Lord delivered him from the hand of all his enemies and from the hand of Saul.

Has the Lord ever rescued you from the hand of an enemy? If so, perhaps the words of David express your own relief and joy:

"I love Thee, O Lord, my strength."
The Lord is my rock and my fortress and my deliverer,
My God, my rock, in whom I take refuge;
My shield and the horn of my salvation, my stronghold.
I call upon the Lord, who is worthy to be praised,
And I am saved from my enemies. (vv. 1–3)

We see ourselves in the lines of David's psalms, as well as the psalms written by other poets such as Moses, Solomon, and Asaph. But most importantly, we see the Lord. When we read the psalms, the Lord lifts the world off our shoulders and returns it to its proper place. Our eyes turn upward, and we praise and worship Him alone.

Like the songs on the radio, the psalms come in a variety of types and styles. There are

- personal psalms (see Pss. 32; 51; and 59)

- historical/teaching psalms (see Ps. 78)

- prophetical/doctrinal psalms (see Pss. 2; 22)

- alphabetical psalms (see Ps. 119, in which the sections are organized according to the letters of the Hebrew alphabet)

Some are majestic songs of worship, some are warnings of

disaster, and some are devotional compositions for quiet meditation.

In our hard-edged, pressure-filled lives, the psalms are soft corners that invite us to rest and recover. When troubles pour down like rain, they put a roof of hope over our heads and give us songs for our hearts to sing.

Solomon, a Pampered Genius Who Drifted Too Far

We enter Solomon's rich forests of wisdom on the next leg of our trip. During his reign as king of Israel, God lavished on him great wisdom; and the poetry of Ecclesiastes, Song of Solomon, and most of Proverbs are the results.

The book of Proverbs is a collection of pithy, brief axioms or statements of truth that differ in style and purpose from the flowing psalms. The following chart lists some of the contrasts.

Psalms	Proverbs
Fellowship with God on the vertical plane	Fellowship with others on the horizontal plane
How to get along with the Lord	How to get along with other people
For our devotional life	For our practical life
Excellent preparation for worship on Sundays	Excellent preparation for work during the week
Theme: Worship	Theme: Wisdom

The bite-sized morsels of truth the book of Proverbs offers usually come in one of three kinds of couplets. Some are *contrastive*, indicated by the word *but*, as in 12:22:

> Lying lips are an abomination to the Lord,
> But those who deal faithfully are His delight.
> (see also vv. 23–27)

Other proverbs are *completive*, with the words *and* or *so* being the key, as in 16:3:

> Commit your works to the Lord,
> And your plans will be established.
> (see also vv. 13, 29)

Finally, others are *comparative*, using the combination *better/than* or *like/so*, as in 15:16–17:

> Better is a little with the fear of the Lord,
> Than great treasure and turmoil with it.

Better is a dish of vegetables where love is,
Than a fattened ox and hatred with it.
(see also 25:25)

Conveniently, they are arranged in thirty-one chapters—just the right number for us to digest one chapter each day of the month! In Ecclesiastes, we get a glimpse into the king's private journal. Here he records his search for happiness apart from God. A billionaire by today's standards, Solomon employed his power and money to explore every alternative path to fulfillment: knowledge, pleasure, possessions, wisdom, and work. However, all his endeavors led him to a dead end.

"Vanity of vanities," says the Preacher,
"Vanity of vanities! All is vanity." (Eccles. 1:2)

Solomon evaluated a God-less life in reality's bare light. The book would leave us despairing but for its hopeful finale:

The conclusion, when all has been heard, is: fear God and keep His commandments, because this applies to every person. For God will bring every act to judgment, everything which is hidden, whether it is good or evil. (12:13–14)

As Ecclesiastes is philosophical, the Song of Solomon is passionate. It's the story of courtship and affection, of love and sexual intimacy between a man and his newlywed bride. Some allegorize the Song of Solomon, identifying Christ as the husband and the church as the bride. But, applying the adage "when normal sense makes the best sense apply no other sense," it's best to take the book at face value as a delightful and romantic love story.

Here's a tip to help you understand who's talking to whom in the book: when you read "my darling," it's usually the husband addressing his wife; "my beloved" is the way the young bride addresses her husband. For example:

"How beautiful you are, *my darling*,
How beautiful you are!
Your eyes are like doves."
"How handsome you are, *my beloved*,
And so pleasant!
Indeed, our couch is luxuriant!
The beams of our houses are cedars,

Our rafters, cypresses."
(1:15-17, emphasis added)

What Can These Biblical Mentors Teach Us?

The poetry of Scripture impresses us with its beauty and color and vivid scenery. As we read the poetical books, we need to let the pictures of worship or despair or romance fill our senses and speak to our humanity. If we get to know the poets themselves, they'll teach us some lasting lessons.

Job, for instance, teaches that *even a genuinely righteous person can suffer terribly*. How we wish that only the wicked and not the innocent would languish in dark prisons of pain. Until the final judgment, however, bad things will happen to good people. Job reminds us of that and offers his hand of sympathy during our suffering.

David teaches us that *even a man after God's heart can fall into tragic sinfulness*. It is hard for us to believe that the same David who could sing glorious praises to the Lord one moment could kiss the forbidden lips of Bathsheba the next. Yet aren't we all just as capable of committing as great a sin as David's? And isn't God just as willing to restore us if we repent?

Solomon teaches us that *even a literary genius can miss some of life's most basic truths*. Solomon may have been the wisest man in the world, but in the end he foolishly gave his heart to idolatrous women. Ironically, his own words tell us,

Watch over your heart with all diligence,
For from it flow the springs of life. (Prov. 4:23)

Are you keeping a close vigil on your heart? Does the Lord have first place in your affections? If He does, you're wiser than King Solomon!

 Living Insights STUDY ONE

"The counsel for the defense may present his case."

"Thank you, your honor. The prosecution charges that my client—the highly-esteemed art of poetry—is out of date in our high-tech age and demands that it be sentenced forever to the lyrics of pop music and greeting cards. Members of the jury (that's you, dear reader), I intend to prove that my client has been maligned and falsely accused. I call to the stand my first witness, the respected theologian Ronald Allen.

"Dr. Allen, please tell the court your opinion of the value of poetry."

> Literature is a language of experience, and poetry is the most concentrated form of literature. Poetry is therefore the most powerful literary means of expressing experience.[3]

"I see. And what kinds of experiences and emotions does poetry help us express, Dr. Allen?"

> How very many times, for example, must Psalm 23 have been recited in funeral settings! Now chanted, now recited by rote; sometimes read with fervor, other times haltingly, with tears blurring the words—the Psalm of the Shepherd will never lose its luster. . . .
>
> In fact, consider any of the familiar lines of the Psalter meditatively, and you will discover how appropriate they are in mirroring the variegated moods of the life of faith. We, who so often find our tongues stammering, our emotions choked, and our minds muddy, find our very necessary expressions of reality in these lines from the Psalms. Whether our mood is blue or bright, whether we question God or confidently trust Him, whether we feel like singing or like weeping; we can do these in the Psalms.[4]

"Your honor, may I impose upon the court a simple test to prove Dr. Allen's thesis concerning the power and relevance of poetry?"

"Proceed, counsel."

"Members of the jury, printed here for you is the psalm to which Dr. Allen referred, Psalm 23. Please read it slowly and thoughtfully. Then, in the space provided, write down its relevance to a certain situation in your life—perhaps how it comforts you or gives you courage. Take your time. You may begin."

3. Allen, *Praise: A Matter of Life and Breath*, p. 43.
4. Allen, *Praise: A Matter of Life and Breath*, pp. 18–20.

The Lord is my shepherd,
I shall not want.
He makes me lie down in green pastures;
He leads me beside quiet waters.
He restores my soul;
He guides me in the paths of righteousness
For His name's sake.
Even though I walk through the valley of the
    shadow of death,
I fear no evil; for Thou art with me;
Thy rod and Thy staff, they comfort me.
Thou dost prepare a table before me in the
    presence of my enemies;
Thou hast anointed my head with oil;
My cup overflows.
Surely goodness and lovingkindness will follow
    me all the days of my life,
And I will dwell in the house of the Lord forever.

_____

_____

_____

_____

_____

_____

_____

_____

"Your honor, the defense rests."

 Living Insights   STUDY TWO

Bidding you to come follow them through the scenic beauty of
their poetry are the three poets—Job, David, and Solomon. Are
you suffering? Take Job's hand. Does your soul long to praise the
Lord? David is your guide. Do you need wisdom? Sit at the feet of

Solomon. Which of these three men would you like to become friends with this month?

❑ Job

❑ David

❑ Solomon

Now design a plan so that you can read a certain amount of that person's poetry every day this month. For instance, you may wish to read through the entire book of Psalms at a pace of five chapters per day. Or you may only want to read David's psalms. By locating the superscription, you'll find seventy-three psalms attributed to David. Reading two or three psalms per day, you can finish them in about a month. Or you may want to read one chapter of Proverbs each day, or work your way slowly through Ecclesiastes and Song of Solomon. Whatever your plan, read with your heart open to receive their generous gift of meaningful words.

My reading plan:

_____

_____

_____

Date completed: _____

Chapter 8

THOSE GRAND OLD BOOKS OF PROPHECY

Survey of Isaiah through Malachi

R oad signs like these must have been common along the section of Route 66 that rolled through the swirling dust bowls of Oklahoma and Texas. Traversing this American Sahara, thousands of cars fell victim to the intense heat, sputtering and wheezing to the side of the road in a cloud of radiator steam. Only the toughest machines made it through.

Such unyielding engines were like the tough-minded prophets of the Bible who endured the heat of a difficult calling. Surviving blistering criticism and fiery threats on their lives, they kept driving onward, determined to speak the word of the Lord no matter what the cost.

To help us understand these courageous and unconventional

people, let's begin with four general facts about their role in Hebrew history.

Some Helpful Reminders about the Prophets

First, keeping this part of God's Route 66 clear in our minds is easier if we understand the difference between a prophet and a priest. *Priests were people's representatives to God, while prophets were God's representatives to people.* If the Hebrews wanted God to forgive their sins, they called out to Him through a priest who offered prayers and sacrifices on their behalf. But if God desired to communicate with them, He spoke through a prophet.

Second, *the prophets' ministry was both forthtelling and foretelling.* Prophets would "tell forth" God's message to the people, firmly revealing to them the truth they needed to hear for today. They would also "foretell" the future, predicting God's judgments as well as His hopeful plan for tomorrow. How could you know whether a prophet was true or false? By the acid test of total accuracy. If even one prophecy missed the bull's-eye, the prophet was discredited as a phony (see Deut. 18:21–22).

Third, *the prophets' primary messages concerned human sin and God's righteousness.* These two themes weave their way through all the prophetical books, as do two others—the people's need to repent and the blessings God would give if they did. The prophets weren't always proclaiming dark oracles of death and doom. Shimmering like silken threads were God's hopeful promises that if the people returned to Him, He would forgive their sins and comfort them.

And fourth, *the prophets' ministries fit into three major sections of Jewish history.*

- The preexilic period: from the dividing of the kingdom to the invasion of the Babylonians

- The exilic period: from the exile of the Jews in Babylon to their return to Jerusalem

- The postexilic period: after the return to Jerusalem, which occurred in three phases under Zerubbabel, Ezra, and Nehemiah

The following chart shows how the prophetical books fit into these three periods.

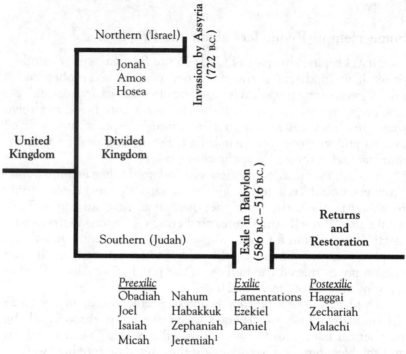

Whatever era they ministered in, the prophets usually weren't appreciated until years later (compare Ezek. 33:30–33). Jeremiah, for example, was imprisoned in the depths of a mud-filled cistern (Jer. 38:1–6), and tradition holds that Isaiah was the one "sawn in two" in Hebrews 11:37. Theologian Leon Wood explains what kind of person could fulfill such a risky calling.

> Prophets had to be people of outstanding character, great minds, and courageous souls. They had to be this by nature and then, being dedicated to God, they became still greater because of the tasks and special provisions assigned them. Thus they became the towering giants of Israel, the formers of public

---

1. Jeremiah's ministry actually spanned two periods, the preexilic and the exilic. Unlike the other Jewish leaders Nebuchadnezzar brought with him to Babylon, Jeremiah remained behind to witness the fall of Jerusalem—which he wrote about in Lamentations—and to accompany the surviving Jews as they later fled to Egypt.

opinion, the leaders through days of darkness, people distinguished from all those about them either in Israel or other nations of the day.[2]

Let's get to know these remarkable men and their writings better.

An Overall Look at the Prophets

Many other prophets traveled the roads of Hebrew history besides the sixteen listed in our Bible's table of contents. There were the more well-known prophets, such as Elijah and Elisha; and some lesser-knowns, such as Nathan, Gad, Jehu, and Shemaiah; as well as the prophetesses Miriam, Deborah, and Huldah. For our purposes, though, let's just look at the writing prophets—the ones who authored the books that have been placed in Scripture.

The Categories . . . and Why We Have Them

We can group these sixteen prophets into two categories:

Major Prophets	Minor Prophets	
Isaiah	Hosea	Nahum
Jeremiah (Lamentations)	Joel	Habakkuk
Ezekiel	Amos	Zephaniah
Daniel	Obadiah	Haggai
	Jonah	Zechariah
	Micah	Malachi

Unlike baseball's major league and minor league, these designations have nothing to do with the importance of the prophets. The relative size of the books and the extensiveness of the messianic prophecies are the only considerations—the major prophets' books are longer and speak more about the coming Christ than those of the minor prophets.[3]

2. Leon J. Wood, *The Prophets of Israel* (Grand Rapids, Mich.: Baker Book House, 1979), p. 16.

3. J. Sidlow Baxter notes, "The twelve writings grouped as the 'Minor Prophets,' though they amplify various aspects, do not determine the main shape of Messianic prophecy. They conform to the general frame already formed for us in Isaiah, Jeremiah, Ezekiel and Daniel." *Explore the Book* (Grand Rapids, Mich.: Zondervan Publishing House, Academie Books, 1960), p. 200. Also, you may notice that both Hosea and Zechariah have more chapters than Daniel, but Daniel's chapters are much longer. That's another reason his book is grouped with the major prophets.

As far as we can tell, all the books were written by the person whose name appears in the title. Some of the prophets open a window into their own lives, like Jonah, whose personal story makes up the whole of the book. Daniel is another who invites us to see God at work in his life; half his book consists of his story while the other half records his prophecies. Isaiah and Jeremiah write mostly of God's messages, adding just a sprinkling of autobiography; while many of the minor prophets record only the word they received from the Lord.

The Prophets . . . Where They Ministered and When

Based on the prophets' own information about themselves, we can get an idea of when they lived and to whom they spoke.

The prophets who ministered in the northern kingdom of Israel were Jonah, Amos, and Hosea (862–725 B.C.). All were preexilic, but that's where their similarity stops. Jonah's reluctant word was not directed to Israel but to one of her enemies—the Assyrian city of Nineveh. Blunt Amos, a fig-picker actually from Judah, withheld none of God's piercing rebukes to Israel, saying, "The Lord God has spoken! Who can but prophesy?" (Amos 3:8b). And Hosea's marriage became his painful sermon, painting the spiritual adultery of God's people in vivid colors.

The southern kingdom of Judah was the preexilic home for eight of the prophets who voiced the word of the Lord from 887 to 586 B.C. They were Isaiah, known as the Prince of Prophets; Jeremiah, the Weeping Prophet; Joel, who warned of the locusts' devastation; Obadiah, who directed his prophecies to neighboring Edom; Micah, who told of the time when swords will be hammered into plowshares; Nahum, another of Nineveh's doomsayers; Habakkuk, decrying the violence of his time yet exalting God for "hinds' feet . . . on my high places" (Hab. 3:19); and Zephaniah, who spoke of the fearsome Day of the Lord.

Then, from 595 to 397 B.C., the exilic and postexilic prophets stepped in. As part of the early group of exiles, Ezekiel and Daniel wrote to reassure the disheartened Jews living in Babylon that God was still in charge of the future. When the Jews were finally allowed to return to Jerusalem and rebuild the temple and the city walls, three postexilic prophets picked up their pens to help rebuild the people's hearts: Haggai, Zechariah, and Malachi.

The prophets came from all walks of life. Some were princes, some farmers, some priests. Some, like Daniel, wore the silks of royalty; while others, like Jeremiah, wore the rags of a prisoner. Some traveled the world, while others knew only their own hometown. But despite their diversity, they all accomplished the same result—they pricked the nation's conscience, making comfortable people feel very uncomfortable in their sin.

How did the people respond? With deep regret and a desire to change? No, rather than getting rid of their sin, the people got rid of the prophets—they smashed the fire alarm instead of dousing the fire. They hunted down the prophets and threw them into prison. They taunted, tortured, and killed them. And when God sent other prophets, they silenced them too. In the end, the house of Israel collapsed in flames.

The Writings . . . and What They Tell Us about the Writers

What kept the prophets going through their deserts of persecution? The same thing that can fuel us to keep speaking the truth during scorching opposition: character. Several qualities of the prophets' character shine through their writings. Let's thumb through some of the books and list a few of these qualities.

- They were uncompromising individualists (see Dan. 1:1–16).

- They were men who stood alone, fully conscious of God's divine calling in their lives (see Jer. 1:4–10).

- They were men of rugged determination (see Ezek. 2:1–7).

- They were men of prayer and untarnished integrity (see Dan. 6:1–10).

- They were outspoken critics of social ills (see Amos 5:10–13; Hab. 1:1–4).

- They were zealous for the things of the Lord (see Hag. 1:2–8).

- They were men who saw and wrote of the coming of the Lord (see Zech. 14:1–11).

A Couple of Remaining Principles to Ponder

The next time you page through your Bible for some inspirational reading, flip to one of the prophetical books. Now that you know a little about the background of the authors, you'll be able to understand them better. As you read, keep in mind the following two principles.

When a prophet brings the warnings of God, his words should prompt the fear of God. Let the message sensitize your spirit to God's commands for your life and give you a hearty respect for the Lord.

When a prophet reveals the will of God, our souls should entertain new dimensions of the plan of God. There's something panoramic about the ministry of the prophets that helps us see the beginning and the end of time. That broad perspective can impact your life today and give you courage to face the challenges of tomorrow.

 Living Insights STUDY ONE

What picture comes to mind when you think of a prophet? Perhaps it's the looming figure of the street-preacher Karl Menninger describes in his book *Whatever Became of Sin?*

> On a sunny day in September, 1972, a stern-faced, plainly dressed man could be seen standing still on a street corner in the busy Chicago Loop. As pedestrians hurried by on their way to lunch or business, he would solemnly lift his right arm, and pointing to the person nearest him, intone loudly the single word "GUILTY!"
>
> Then, without any change of expression, he would resume his stiff stance for a few moments before repeating the gesture. Then, again, the inexorable raising of his arm, the pointing, and the solemn pronouncing of the one word "GUILTY!"
>
> The effect of this strange *j'accuse* pantomime on the passing strangers was extraordinary, almost eerie. They would stare at him, hesitate, look away, look at each other, and then at him again; then hurriedly continue on their ways.
>
> One man, turning to another who was my informant, exclaimed: "But how did *he* know?"
>
> No doubt many others had similar thoughts. How *did* he know, indeed?
>
> "Guilty!" *Everyone* guilty? Guilty of what? Guilty of overparking? Guilty of lying? Guilty of arrogance and hubris toward the one God? Guilty of "borrowing," not to say embezzling? Guilty of unfaithfulness

78

to a faithful wife? Guilty only of evil thoughts—or evil plans?[4]

If that is your image of a prophet, you are right. Prophets did stand up to commoners and kings alike, pointing their bony fingers of judgment. "Guilty!" they would announce, like Nathan before adulterous David. "You are the man!" he cried, slamming down God's gavel of guilt (2 Sam. 12:7).

But prophets had a more tender side too. "The Lord also has taken away your sin; you shall not die," breathed Nathan after hearing David's confession (v. 13). And when Solomon, Bathsheba's second child by David, was born, it was Nathan, like a doting godfather, who called him Jedidiah—"beloved of the Lord" (see vv. 24–25).

Do not fear the prophets. Do not run from them, covering your head in shame. As your read their books, open your heart to their words. Let them do their cleansing work in your soul, and feel God's tender touch of forgiveness.

 Living Insights   STUDY TWO

How far would you go to communicate God's words of warning to your friends? Would you call them on the phone? Write them a letter? Travel a hundred miles? Certainly!

But suppose they don't listen. To really get the message across, would you shave your head? Would you lay on your left side for 390 days? Would you eat bread baked over cow dung?

Well . . .

These are the lengths to which God told Ezekiel to go in order to tell the exiled Jews of Jerusalem's destruction (see Ezek. 4:1–5:12). Of course, God isn't asking us to do strange stunts like these. But it makes us think, *What sacrifices of love would we make to communicate the truth to our friends?*

Perhaps you know someone who is making wrong choices and heading for disaster. You've tried warning him or her, but to no avail. Could now be the right time to try again? Is God calling you to be His prophet's voice in their life? If so, how can you confront them in a way that shows your love for them, on the one hand,

---

4. Karl Menninger, *Whatever Became of Sin?* (New York, N.Y.: Bantam Books, 1973), pp. 1–2.

and the seriousness of their sin on the other? What should you say?

_____

_____

_____

Before you put on the prophet's garb, double-check your motives. Make sure there are no logs in your eye before pointing out the specks in your friend's eye. Ask the Lord to cleanse your heart of any judgmental attitudes. Be prepared to keep loving your friend, whether he or she listens to you or turns away. Only then will you be a prophet in the truest sense.

Chapter 9

FOUR CENTURIES OF
SILENCE

Daniel 2:31–33, 36–40; 7:1–8

W e've been having a great trip so far! The car is running cool and quiet, we've got plenty of snacks left, and the scenery has been magnificent. We've met the patriarchs, the Hebrew nation's founding fathers—Abraham, Isaac, Jacob, and Joseph— etched into Genesis like our presidents in Mount Rushmore. The history-makers of the Old Testament rose before us like giant redwoods, men such as Moses, Aaron, Joshua, and Caleb, the judges Samson and Samuel, and Saul, the first king of Israel.

Crisp, clean mountain air and great, green meadows greeted us when we reached the poets, Job, David, and Solomon. And most recently we traveled the rugged terrain of the prophets, beginning with Isaiah and stretching across centuries to Malachi.

More than two thousand years of history spreads behind us like a giant patchwork quilt . . . and our journey isn't over yet. The life of Christ and Mount Calvary still lie ahead.

So let's get go— Wait! Watch out! What in the world has happened to our road? There's a huge chasm here between us and the New Testament. How can that be? The New Testament is just a flip of the page from the Old Testament in our Bibles . . . except for this blank page in between. Let's see what a history brochure has to say about this.

Hmmm. Here it is. This is known as the intertestamental period. During this time, dark clouds hovered overhead, forming a curtain across the heavens. Not one prophet spoke the word of the Lord. Not one poet filled the air with inspired prayer. Not one God-ordained historian sat down to record world events for Scripture. For four centuries, God was silent.

But He wasn't absent.

Quietly, He was working behind the scenes, forming nations, moving the hearts of kings, and preparing the world for the arrival of His Son. Eventually, according to the apostle Paul,

> *when the fullness of the time came,* God sent forth His
> Son, born of a woman, born under the Law, in order

that He might redeem those who were under the Law, that we might receive the adoption as sons. (Gal. 4:4–5, emphasis added)

What brought about "the fullness of the time"? Our portion of God's Route 66 has stopped short, and without the guide of Scripture, how can we find our way to the other side?

The prophets, you say? Good idea. Maybe one of them foretold of this time. Let's see . . . here we go. Daniel. It looks like Daniel mapped out several key events that will lead us from his day in the exilic period through the intertestamental chasm to Christ. So let's shift into four-wheel drive and hit the trail with Daniel's prophetic map.

Two Dreams in Daniel

Daniel sees the future through the telescopes of two dreams that at first seem unrelated. The first comes to the Babylonian king, Nebuchadnezzar.

Nebuchadnezzar's Dream (Daniel 2)

More like a nightmare, the king's dream torments him so that "his spirit was troubled and his sleep left him" (Dan. 2:1b). Calling in the court seers, the king demands not only that they interpret the dream but that they recount to him the dream itself. This would guarantee that they were true prophets and that their interpretation could be trusted.

Of course, no one can solve the riddle. When Daniel hears of the situation—and the king's threat to kill all the wise men in Babylon—he prays that God would have compassion and tell him the dream. God does, and "the mystery was revealed to Daniel in a night vision." Confidently, then, he approaches Nebuchadnezzar with these words:

> "You, O king, were looking and behold, there was a single great statue; that statue, which was large and of extraordinary splendor, was standing in front of you, and its appearance was awesome. The head of that statue was made of fine gold, its breast and its arms of silver, its belly and its thighs of bronze, its legs of iron, its feet partly of iron and partly of clay." (vv. 31–33)

As the dream continued, a stone suddenly struck the feet of the statue, collapsing the structure into a heap. The metal pieces became like chaff, and the wind blew them away until nothing was left. Then the stone grew into a great mountain, filling the whole earth (vv. 34–35).[1]

That's the king's dream, all right. But what does it mean?

In verses 37–40, Daniel identifies the four parts of the statue as four empires. The golden head is Nebuchadnezzar's Babylonian Empire. The silver chest and arms represent the Medes and the Persians, two nations that later join forces to overthrow the Babylonians (see chap. 5).[2]

The Old Testament ends during the reign of the Medes and the Persians, but Daniel's prophecy doesn't stop here. The bronze belly and thighs represent the Greek Empire of Alexander the Great, who ruled "over all the earth" during the intertestamental period (2:39b). Last, the legs and feet of iron and the iron corrupted with clay portray the powerful but eventually deteriorating Roman Empire that tromped across the Greek-ruled world.

Daniel's interpretation of the dream so accurately predicts the rise and fall of world powers that many scholars have concluded that he must have written the prophecy *after* the events took place. But, as the astonished Nebuchadnezzar recognizes, God is "a revealer of mysteries" (v. 47b). He can see the future as if it were yesterday, and He has another dream in store, this time for His prophet Daniel.

Daniel's Dream (Daniel 7)

In the first year of Belshazzar king of Babylon Daniel saw a dream and visions in his mind as he lay on his bed; then he wrote the dream down and related the following summary of it. Daniel said, "I was looking in my vision by night, and behold, the four winds of heaven were stirring up the great sea.

---

1. J. Dwight Pentecost identifies the stone as the Messiah, Jesus Christ, who will conquer future world governments and establish His kingdom on earth at His second coming (see also vv. 44–45). See "Daniel," in *The Bible Knowledge Commentary*, Old Testament ed., ed. John F. Walvoord and Roy B. Zuck (Wheaton, Ill.: Scripture Press Publications, Victor Books, 1985), p. 1336.

2. The events in the postexilic books of Esther, Ezra, and Nehemiah take place during the time of the Medo-Persian Empire.

And four great beasts were coming up from the sea, different from one another." (7:1–3)

Instead of a statue with four parts, four animals enter the gates of Daniel's mind.

"The first was like a lion and had the wings of an eagle. I kept looking until its wings were plucked, and it was lifted up from the ground and made to stand on two feet like a man; a human mind also was given to it." (v. 4)

Interestingly, the description of this strange lion mirrors an incident in Nebuchadnezzar's life. According to Daniel 4, the king was boasting about his power and majesty when the Lord touched his mind, causing him to go mad. He began grazing in the field like an animal walking on all fours, and

his body was drenched with the dew of heaven, until his hair had grown like *eagles' feathers* and his nails like birds' claws. (v. 33b, emphasis added)

When the king finally honored the Lord as the King of heaven, he stood up on two feet, his reason returned to him, and God restored his splendor and power. The parallel between Nebuchadnezzar and the proud lion that had its wings plucked and was lifted up on two feet and given a "human mind" is too close to be a coincidence—the lion represents Nebuchadnezzar and his Babylonian Empire.

Daniel's dream continues:

"And behold, another beast, a second one, resembling a bear. And it was raised up on one side, and three ribs were in its mouth between its teeth; and thus they said to it, 'Arise, devour much meat!'" (7:5)

The second animal, signifying the Medo-Persian Empire, is a bear "raised up on one side"—a depiction of the Persians' superiority over their Median allies. The three ribs in its mouth and the command, "Arise, devour much meat!" represents the three nations the Medes and Persians vanquished—Babylon, Lydia, and Egypt—and the land they "devour" in their pursuit of world domination.

Next comes a third animal:

"After this I kept looking, and behold, another one, like a leopard, which had on its back four wings of a bird; the beast also had four heads, and dominion was given to it." (v. 6)

The four-winged leopard represents the quickness and strength of Alexander the Great. While still a young man, he had led his Greek army to victory after victory, conquering the world with amazing speed. After he died, four of his generals divvied up the empire—symbolized by the four heads of the leopard. Cassander took Macedonia; Lysimachus, Asia Minor; Seleucus, Syria; and Ptolemy, Egypt.

With the entrance of the fourth beast, the dream turns nightmarish:

"After this I kept looking in the night visions, and behold, a fourth beast, dreadful and terrifying and extremely strong; and it had large iron teeth. It devoured and crushed, and trampled down the remainder with its feet; and it was different from all the beasts that were before it, and it had ten horns." (v. 7)

This terrifying beast is different from the other animal-like creatures. Brutal and greedy, it brings to mind the merciless Roman legions, the Iron Empire, as it trampled its foes and consumed the territories left by Alexander's successors.

So, as we can now see, both Nebuchadnezzar's and Daniel's dreams have the same interpretation. The following chart shows just how they correspond.

Nebuchadnezzar's Dream		Daniel's Dream	Interpretation
Body Part	Element	Animal/Beast	World Kingdom
head	gold	lion	Babylonian Empire
chest, arms	silver	bear	Medo-Persian Empire
belly, thighs	bronze	leopard	Greek Empire
legs, feet	iron and iron/clay	terrible beast	Roman Empire

Also, note the similarity between the ten toes on the statue and the ten horns on the fourth beast. Commentator J. Dwight Pentecost helps us understand what this means.

The fourth empire, in spite of its great power (vv. 7, 23), will be characterized by progressive weakness, deterioration, and division. . . . When the hordes from the north conquered the Roman Empire in the fifth century A.D., they did not unite to form another empire. Instead individual nations emerged out of the old Roman Empire. Some of those nations and others stemming from them have continued till the present day. The present Age, then, is the 10-horned era of the fourth beast.[3]

The ten horns particularly intrigued Daniel. As he watched, something new appeared in his dream—something without parallel in Nebuchadnezzar's:

> "Another horn, a little one, came up among them, and three of the first horns were pulled out by the roots before it; and behold, this horn possessed eyes like the eyes of a man, and a mouth uttering great boasts." (v. 8)

The little horn—or king (see v. 24)—who grows out of the rest is the Antichrist. According to verse 25, he will arrogantly defy God, persecute the saints, and rule for "a time, times, and half a time," or three and a half years (see also Rev. 13:5). As accurate as Daniel is concerning Babylon, Medo-Persia, Greece, and Rome, we can be sure that he will be just as correct concerning the future Antichrist's rise to power and, thankfully, his fall when Christ comes to reign.

Significant Events during the Intertestamental Period

Through misty visions, Daniel could see the brightest events in the intertestamental chasm. As we drive through these four hundred years of history, the details become even clearer.

Six Flags over Israel

During this period, six flags of six governments fly over Israel. Here are the nations' names and dates:

• Medo-Persian rule   536–333 B.C.

---

3. Pentecost, "Daniel," p. 1354. He continues: "Other premillennialists, however, hold that the time of the 10 horns is yet future, that the present Church Age is not seen in this vision, and that 10 kings will coexist over a future revived (or realigned) Roman Empire."

- Grecian rule   333–323 B.C.
- Egyptian rule   323–204 B.C.
- Syrian rule   204–165 B.C.
- Maccabean rule   165–63 B.C.
- Roman rule   63 B.C. through the New Testament

God enlists these governments to help Him set the stage for the entrance of His Son. Alexander the Great unites the world with the trade language of Koine Greek so everyone can understand the words of Christ, and Rome builds the roads for missionaries to travel and spread the gospel.

Four Faces of Authority

Also during this era, four faces of authority emerge in Palestine that will play significant roles in the New Testament: the Pharisees and scribes—superspiritual religious separatists; the Sanhedrin—the Jewish supreme court; the Sadducees—the priestly upper class who cling to their political clout from Rome; and the Herodians—those who support Herod and his Rome-backed dynasty.

Three Facts about Scripture

Finally, concerning the Scriptures, three significant events occur. First, the Old Testament is compiled and preserved as the thirty-nine books we have today. Second, the Septuagint is completed around 250 B.C. This is the Greek translation of the Hebrew Bible, which put the Scriptures in the common language of the people, opening the Bible of the Old Testament to people of the New Testament era. And third, the Apocrypha is penned—a collection of noncanonical writings that give us a glimpse into history and the influence of Greek culture on Jewish thought.[4]

A Final Word

This canyon of the "silent" years between the Old and New Testaments echoes one truth loud and clear: God is sovereign. Are

---

4. The books of the Apocrypha are 1 and 2 Esdras, Tobit, Judith, Additions to Esther (or The Rest of Esther), The Wisdom of Solomon, Ecclesiasticus (or the Wisdom of Jesus Son of Sirach), Baruch, Prayer of Azariah and the Song of the Three Holy Children, Susanna, Bel and the Dragon, The Prayer of Manasseh, and 1 and 2 Maccabees.

you traveling through an uncharted canyon? Have dark clouds of doubt drawn themselves like curtains in front of the heavens? Remember, even though God seems silent, He is not absent. The drama of history bears out His pervasive presence, and He is at work behind the scenes of your life too.

 Living Insights

Sometimes in life we strain to listen for God's clear voice, but all we hear is silence. We yearn to feel the strong arm of God's presence, but all we sense is air. At those times, it is good to remember the story of Esther.

> More than any other biblical book, Esther is a tribute to the invisible providence of God. Although we never actually hear or see God in the story, we have an overwhelming sense of confidence that He is just offstage, cueing the characters and orchestrating the drama to preserve His people from a tragic ending.
> The Book of Esther is often like the dramas played out in our everyday lives. For seldom when enemies are on our heels are our Red Seas parted. Seldom when disaster is at our door are we warned by angelic visitors. Seldom when we are in need of direction are we instructed by God from a burning bush. And neither was Esther.
> It's easy to see God in the miraculous. It's not so easy to see Him in the mundane. But that's where most of us live. We live without seeing handwriting on the wall or hearing thunder from Sinai. We live with God not center stage but directing unobtrusively from the wings.[5]

Under God's direction, Esther went from obscurity to become the queen of Persia and then to play the lead role in saving the Jews from Haman's plot to annihilate them. All this God did without

---

5. From the study guide *Esther: A Woman for Such a Time as This*, coauthored by Ken Gire, from the Bible-teaching ministry of Charles R. Swindoll (Fullerton, Calif.: Insight for Living, 1990), p. 1.

one trumpet call from heaven or one vision in the night. Instead, He used ordinary events of daily life—an open door, a word of advice, a crossing of paths, a willing heart, a wise approach.

Are you waiting for God to part the Red Sea or write a message on the wall before you make a certain decision? If you are traveling through a chasm of divine silence in your life, could God be directing you even though you don't hear His voice?

Take a few moments to jot down any open doors, words of advice, or crossing of paths God may be using to guide you. Don't forget to include key verses He is showing you as well. Through these clues and cues, what action could God be directing you to take?

Clues: _____

_____

_____

Action: _____

_____

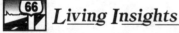 *Living Insights*   STUDY TWO

Congratulations! We've reached a milestone . . . the end of the Old Testament. It's hard to believe we've traveled all the way from the dawn of creation to the rise of the Roman Empire. The B.C.s are behind us now. Are you ready for the A.D.s?

While we're refueling, why don't we wave good-bye to the Old Testament with a quick review? I know, you're anxious to get going, but we have a little time. Here's a nickel for a cold Grape Nehi. Rest yourself a minute, and see how well you can fill in the blanks.[6]

1. Genesis is the book of _____.

2. List four major events in the book of Genesis.

_____   _____

_____   _____

---

6. The answers are provided after the "Books for Probing Further" section at the end of the guide.

3. List four major people in the book of Genesis.

_____   _____

_____   _____

4. The book of _____ is the story of the Hebrew nation's deliverance from Egyptian bondage.

5. Israel's worship manual is the book of _____.

6. The book of Numbers chronicles Israel's _____ through the wilderness.

7. "Remember" was the theme of the sermons Moses preached to the Hebrew people in the book of _____.

8. The conquest of the Promised Land is the subject of the book of _____.

9. Defeat and compromise lay ahead for the Israelites in the book of _____.

10. The pure pearl on the black backdrop of Judges is this book about committed love: _____.

11. First Samuel 1 through 1 Kings 11 records the history of the _____ kingdom.

12. The first three kings of Israel were:

_____ _____ _____.

13. The five poetical books are:_____ _____

_____ _____ _____.

14. First Kings 12 through 2 Chronicles 36 records the history of the _____ kingdom.

15. After the nation split, the northern kingdom was called _____ and the southern kingdom was called _____.

16. The three prophets to the north were Jonah, Amos, and _____.

17. In 722 B.C., the northern kingdom was destroyed by the _____.

18. In 586 B.C., the southern kingdom was destroyed by the
_____.

19. The two major prophets who ministered to the exiled Jews in Babylon were _____ and _____.

20. The Jews returned to Palestine in three groups. The first band was led by Zerubbabel; the second, Ezra; and the third,
_____.

21. The period between the Old and New Testaments lasted _____ years.

Finished already? Great! The tank is full, the windows are clean, and the engine is humming. Let's hit the road!

Chapter 10
WHY FOUR GOSPELS?
Survey of the Gospels

The intertestamental chasm fades in our rearview mirror as we rejoin God's Route 66 in the New Testament and cruise into the Gospels: Matthew, Mark, Luke, and John. Named for their authors, each of these books paints a detailed portrait of Jesus Christ. So, because we're in a hurry, we'll just pick one of them and . . .

That's not a good idea, you say? But what's the use of covering the same ground four times? This is a survey—we need to keep moving.

You say each author may paint Christ's life from a different perspective? And if we put them all together, we'd have a more complete picture of Him?

Well, I suppose you're right. Then let's plan to follow all four writers through the life of Christ simultaneously.

A Helpful Chart of the Gospels

To help distinguish each book from the other, let's summarize their unique slants in an overview chart.[1]

	Matthew	Mark	Luke	John
Portrait	Mighty King	Humble Servant	True Humanity	Absolute Deity
Addressee	The Jews	The Romans	The Greeks	The World
Theme	Royalty and Authority of the King	Work and Service of the Servant	Jesus as Man	Jesus as God
Key Verse	Matthew 21:4–5	Mark 10:45	Luke 19:10	John 20:31

We can see already that each of the writers had in mind different purposes and audiences. None attempted to videotape Jesus' life from start to finish; rather, they took snapshots of various scenes, editing and arranging them according to specific themes.

Since the accounts are not identical, some critics have accused the authors of contradicting one another. Differences, however, don't necessarily mean disagreement. For example, if four people

---

1. Although Matthew appears first in our Bibles, Mark was probably written first, then Luke, then Matthew, and finally John.

stood on the four corners of an intersection and witnessed the same car accident, their stories would differ according to their points of view—but all the facts would still be accurate.

In the same way, because the gospel writers wrote about Christ from various angles, we should expect their stories to differ too. Moreover, if they were exactly the same, we'd probably wonder if they copied each other and question their reliability. Rather than dispute their authenticity, the variations between the accounts actually support it. Let's get a brief feel for some of the distinctions of each gospel.

Matthew

Examining the chart a little more closely, we notice that Matthew paints Christ as a mighty king, dressed in royal robes, full of authority. A Jew himself, Matthew writes to a Jewish audience and includes Jesus' genealogy to prove that He is the Messiah, a descendant of David from the line of Abraham. Because it is vital for his readers to know the ways Jesus fulfills prophecy, Matthew quotes the Old Testament more than any of the other gospel writers. A quotation from Isaiah, in fact, is the key verse of his book. It appears in chapter 21—the section that describes Jesus' kingly entrance into Jerusalem the week before His crucifixion:

> Now this took place that what was spoken through
> the prophet might be fulfilled, saying,
> "Say to the daughter of Zion,
> 'Behold your King is coming to you,
> Gentle, and mounted on a donkey,
> Even on a colt, the foal of a beast of burden.'"
> (vv. 4–5)

Mark

In contrast, Mark portrays Jesus as a humble servant. He doesn't include a genealogy, because his Roman readers would not be interested in a servant's family history—they would want to see Jesus' strength and character. So, rather than dwelling on unfamiliar Hebrew prophecies and long discourses, he packs a lot of action into his brief gospel.[2] The key verse in the book sums up Mark's theme well:

2. In keeping with his fast-action narrative, Mark's favorite word is *immediately*—appearing forty times in the New American Standard Bible.

"For even the Son of Man did not come to be served, but to serve, and to give His life a ransom for many." (10:45)

Luke

The third writer is Luke, a Greek physician who addresses a Greek audience. His readers appreciate achievement, beauty, culture, and large ideas. With all the human drama of a Rembrandt portrait, then, he depicts Jesus as the ideal man. Thoughtfully, he sketches in the subtle details of Christ's life—His genealogy tracing Him back to Adam, His birth, His childhood, His relationships, and His suffering. He highlights more of Jesus' teachings than the other writers, featuring the cherished stories of the Good Samaritan and the Prodigal Son. As displayed in this book's key verse, Jesus' compassion for fallen humanity emanates from Luke's gospel:

"For the Son of Man has come to seek and to save that which was lost." (19:10)

John

Writing years after the other authors completed their works, John dips quill in ink to draw an inspiring portrait of Christ's deity. A king, a servant, an ideal man—Jesus is all that, but even more, He is God. Addressing the whole world with this message, John presents a masterful defense of Jesus' deity, selecting seven signs that prove beyond a doubt that Jesus is the Son of God. These miraculous signs include:

- changing water into wine (2:1–11)

- healing the royal official's son (4:46–54)

- healing the man by the pool of Bethesda (5:1–9a)

- feeding the five thousand (6:5–14)

- walking on the water (6:16–21)

- healing a man born blind (9:1–7)

- raising Lazarus from the dead (11:1–45)

Like any work of art, John's gospel stirs a response in us. Either we accept Jesus as God's Son and receive life, or we reject Him and wander into death. The book's key verse expresses the author's passionate hope concerning the choice we would make:

> Many other signs therefore Jesus also performed in the presence of the disciples, which are not written in this book; but these have been written that you may believe that Jesus is the Christ, the Son of God; and that believing you may have life in His name. (20:30–31)

A Few Clarifying Remarks about the Gospels

Now that we recognize some of the distinguishing characteristics of the Gospels, it's easier to tell them apart. Before we take our tour of them, though, let's rummage through the glove box for a few more facts to help us along the way.

First, *Matthew, Mark, and Luke are known as the Synoptic Gospels.* The word *synoptic* literally means "seen together" (*sýn*—"together"; *ópsis*—"view").[3] They are grouped together because of their similar viewpoints on Christ's life. The fourth gospel, John, is unique. It was written much later and includes information not found in the other gospels—such as the private words of Jesus to the disciples the night before He was crucified (see chaps. 13–17, commonly known as the Upper Room Discourse). Unlike Matthew, John provides us no genealogy; unlike Mark, no emphasis on action; and unlike Luke, no parables. John, as a writer, is more profound and deep. So his book is not put in the same category as the synoptics.

Second, *the Gospels were never intended to give us a complete and uninterrupted story of Jesus' life.* According to John, even if they wanted to, they couldn't.

> And there are also many other things which Jesus did, which if they were written in detail, I suppose that even the world itself would not contain the books which were written. (21:25)

Third, *to study the Gospels thoroughly, we need to "harmonize" them.* Reading the Gospels is like listening to a choir. If you want to hear just the high part, you can sit in the soprano section. Or

---

3. F. V. Filson, "Gospels, Synoptic," in *The International Standard Bible Encyclopedia*, gen. ed. Geoffrey W. Bromiley (Grand Rapids, Mich.: William B. Eerdmans Publishing Co., 1982), vol. 2, p. 532.

to experience the other singers' perspectives, you can sit with the altos or tenors or basses. But the best seat for absorbing the full impact of the music is in the center of the auditorium, where you can hear all the parts harmonizing together. In a similar way, by blending the four gospels together, "harmonizing" the different perspectives on the same story, we can experience the full impact of Jesus' life.

But reading the Gospels that way requires a lot of flipping back and forth from one account to the next, doesn't it? Fortunately, scholars have prepared harmonies of the Gospels for us—books that conveniently display the accounts side by side and in chronological order.[4]

Fourth, *the gospel accounts include the same general outline.* Some Bible teachers outline the life of Christ geographically, walking along with Him as He traverses the land of Palestine. Others arrange the events in Christ's life around a central theme, such as the kingdom of God. But all the outlines follow the same general flow of events, which we will explore next.

Tracing the Major Events through the Gospels

The best place to start is the beginning. With Christ, however, the beginning is not so obvious.

Jesus Christ's Existence before Time Began

The first three gospels pick up the story of Jesus' life in the womb of a young girl named Mary. John, however, reaches farther back in time in search of Christ's origins.

> In the beginning was the Word, and the Word
> was with God, and the Word was God. He was in
> the beginning with God. (1:1–2)

Literally, he says, "In *a* beginning," leaving out the definite article *the*. The implication is that the Word existed before time, "in a beginning that never had a beginning."[5] A few verses later,

---

4. The standard harmony is *A Harmony of the Gospels for Students of the Life of Christ*, by A. T. Robertson (New York, N.Y.: Harper and Row, Publishers, 1950). Robert L. Thomas and Stanley N. Gundry have updated Robertson's work in *The NIV Harmony of the Gospels* (San Francisco, Calif.: Harper and Row, Publishers, 1988).

5. In a discussion with the Pharisees, Jesus Himself claimed to exist prior to His birth. He said, "Truly, truly, I say to you, before Abraham was born, I am" (John 8:58).

John identifies the "Word":

> And the Word became flesh, and dwelt among us, and we beheld His glory, glory as of the only begotten from the Father, full of grace and truth. (v. 14)

The Word is Jesus Christ, who always existed and who created us and the world we live in (see v. 3). John calls Him the Word because He communicated the deepest thoughts and innermost feelings of God in a way we could all understand, by coming and living among us.

His Coming and Living among Humanity

John says that Jesus "dwelt," or, literally, "tabernacled" with us. He pitched his tent on Earth; then, about thirty years later, He pulled up stakes and returned to His home in heaven. As God, He could have come to us in any form He chose, as a brilliant light or a thundering voice. Instead, "the Word became flesh."

"Incarnation" is the term Bible teachers use to describe Jesus' entrance onto Earth's stage, the moment the Son of God became a man. Make no mistake about it, He was fully human. When He hurt, He wept; when He was cut, He bled; when He was tired, He slept. He felt the full range of human emotions, from compassion to rage, from elation to grief. In every way, He was just like us . . . we should say, in every way but one—He never sinned.[6] The perfect, unblemished Lamb of God, Jesus was the only One qualified to be slain on the altar for our sins.

Our Lord's Suffering and Death in our Place

At the apex of each gospel stands the Cross. Dare we rush by this holy place without pausing in solemn wonder? Here the Son of God stretched Himself on a torturous altar of wood and suffered for the sins of the world. Because of their significance to our lives and to the message of Scripture, we'll stop to examine Jesus' final day on earth and His momentous death in the next two chapters.

---

6. Because of Jesus' divine nature, it was impossible for Him to sin. Yet He still experienced the full force of temptation's fury (see Matt. 4:1–11 and Heb. 4:15–16). For a more complete discussion of whether Jesus could or could not sin, see *The Moody Handbook of Theology*, by Paul Enns (Chicago, Ill.: Moody Press, 1989), pp. 236–38.

The Savior's Resurrection and Ascension from Earth

As the Gospels come to a close, the sky brightens with the colors of a new day. The grave cannot hold the Son of God for long, and like the sun's rays, He bursts forth from the darkness of the tomb triumphant and glorious. All four gospel writers revel in this magnificent event, underscoring two facts: Jesus rose bodily—not just in His spirit; and He rose miraculously—His body was not stolen away as some were claiming (see Matt. 28; Mark 16; Luke 24; John 20).

Only Mark and Luke tell us what happens next, and then just briefly. Jesus leaves the earth to take His rightful place by the Father's side (see Mark 16:19; Luke 24:51). In the book of Acts, Luke fills in the details, saying that while the disciples watched, "a cloud received Him out of their sight" (1:9b). Then two angels appeared beside them and said:

> "Men of Galilee, why do you stand looking into the sky? This Jesus, who has been taken up from you into heaven, will come in just the same way as you have watched Him go into heaven." (Acts 1:11)

The King Returns as Ruler over Earth

Today, we're still looking for Christ to part the clouds and step from heaven to Earth once more. Jesus taught that His return would be unexpected and sudden, "just as the lightning comes from the east, and flashes even to the west" (Matt. 24:27). Years later, Jesus showed John in a vision what His coming will be like, and John recorded what he saw in the book of Revelation. Someday, Christ will come again not as a mere man but as King of Kings and Lord of Lords. What a day that will be!

 Living Insights STUDY ONE

Do you long to know Jesus more deeply? The desire to know Christ possessed the nineteenth-century preacher C. H. Spurgeon, who cried out,

> As the river seeks the sea, so Jesus, I seek thee! O let me find thee and melt my life into thine forever![7]

7. C. H. Spurgeon, quoted in *Spurgeon at His Best*, comp. Tom Carter (Grand Rapids, Mich.: Baker Book House, 1988), p. 109.

Is that your desire too? The Gospels were written so that you may know Jesus and, in knowing Him, believe in Him. Has it been awhile since you've read the Gospels? If so, Matthew is calling you to come follow him; Mark is bidding you come as well, and so are Luke and John. Won't you let them be your guides to knowing Christ and trusting Him more? Make a plan now to read a little every day as you stroll down the road with Christ, taking your time to get to know your Savior.

As you follow the biblical authors, invite a modern writer to go along with you. We recommend the following author and his books as amiable traveling companions:

Gire, Ken. *Intimate Moments with the Savior.* Grand Rapids, Mich.: Zondervan Publishing House, 1989.

————. *Incredible Moments with the Savior.* Grand Rapids, Mich.: Zondervan Publishing House, 1990.

————. *Instructive Moments with the Savior.* Grand Rapids, Mich.: Zondervan Publishing House, 1992.

 Living Insights STUDY TWO

Why four gospels? J. Sidlow Baxter summed up the answer best with an illustration.

> Some time ago I was visiting a friend whose wife had recently died. On a cabinet in his sitting-room there was a satin-wood, gold-embroidered, quadri-folding photograph-holder, standing concavely to the room and containing four coloured pictures of his lost loved-one. He explained that those four gave him just the characteristic expressions which were dearest to him. No one photograph was enough— all four were needed. Sometimes this one, and sometimes that one, spoke most to him, but each in its own way brought a flood of affecting memories to his mind.[8]

8. J. Sidlow Baxter, *Explore the Book* (Grand Rapids, Mich.: Zondervan Publishing House, Academie Books, 1960), p. 118.

In the same way, no one account of Jesus' life is enough. We need all four to bring to mind the many wonderful attributes of Christ. In the following four-fold picture frame, write down the features about each gospel you can recall from the lesson. Imagine Christ's picture in each frame as the gospel writer presents Him, and recall that image whenever you read from that gospel in the days to come.

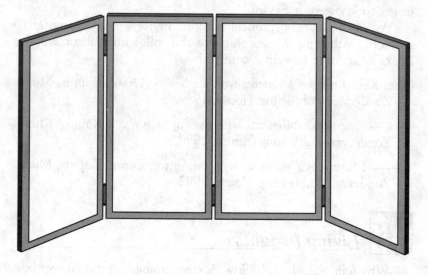

Chapter 11

A CLOSER LOOK AT JESUS' ARREST AND TRIALS

Selected Scriptures

In our trip through the Bible, we've not taken the time to pull over and linger in any one place. Now, however, we've come to a portion of Scripture that we cannot pass by with a mere glance and a wave. We must stop and cover this sacred ground on foot, pausing reflectively to read each marker along the path. Pilgrims from around the world come to embrace the memory of what happened here. Let's join them as we slowly walk through the events surrounding the arrest, trials, and, in the next chapter, the crucifixion of Jesus.

The Matter of Time

Understanding the timing of Jesus' arrest and trials can be confusing—unless we have a firm grasp of the way time was reckoned then. The beginning and ending of the New Testament era's twenty-four-hour day was different from ours. While our day goes from midnight to midnight, their day went from 6:00 in the evening to 6:00 the following evening.

The way their nights and days were divided was also unique. The time of night was told not in hours but in *watches*, which were three-hour periods. Nighttime, then, had four watches: the "first watch," 6 to 9 P.M.; the "second watch," 9 P.M. to midnight; the "third watch," midnight to 3 A.M.; and the "fourth watch," 3 to 6 A.M. Daytime began at 6 A.M. and was divided into twelve individual hours. So, for example, the "third hour" would be 9 A.M., and the "ninth hour" would be 3 P.M.

Knowing these distinctions will help us realize more fully how relentlessly cruel Jesus' last day was.

This chapter has been adapted from the chapters "Arrest and Trial" and "Rush to Judgment" in the study guide *Beholding Christ . . . The Lamb of God: A Study of John 15–21* (Fullerton, Calif.: Insight for Living, 1987), as well as "What Then Shall I Do with Jesus?" from the study guide *Issues and Answers in Jesus' Day* (Fullerton, Calif.: Insight for Living, 1990). Both guides were coauthored by Ken Gire and are from the Bible-teaching ministry of Charles R. Swindoll.

Chronology of Events

Like the furious white water of swift rapids, Jesus' enemies hurl Him into one crashing boulder after another, with no relief, no time to catch His breath and recover.

Event	Approximate Time
Prayer and agony at Gethsemane (Matthew, Mark, Luke)	1:00 A.M.
Betrayal by Judas and arrest of Jesus (Mark 14:43–46; John 18:12)	1:30 A.M.
Irregular, unauthorized inquiry at Annas' residence (John 18:13–23)	2:00 A.M.
Unofficial trial at Caiaphas' residence (Matthew 26:57–68; John 18:24)	3:30 A.M.
Formal, official trial before Sanhedrin in their chamber to confirm capital sentence (Mark 15:1; Luke 22:66–71)	6:00 A.M. ("when it was day")
First interrogation by Pilate at official residence (Matthew 27:1–2, 11–14; Luke 23:1–7; John 18:28–38)	6:30 A.M. ("when morning had come . . . and it was early")
Audience/mockery before Herod (Luke 23:8–12)	7:00 A.M.
Final judgment of Pilate (All Gospels)	7:30 A.M.
Scourging in Praetorium (All Gospels)	8:00 A.M.
Nailing of hands and feet to the cross (All Gospels)	9:00 A.M. ("it was the third hour")
Darkness (Matthew, Mark, Luke)	12:00 Noon ("when the sixth hour had come, darkness fell")
Death of Jesus (All Gospels)	3:00 P.M. ("and at the ninth hour")

In less than twenty-four hours, Jesus goes from arrest to execution.

Trials of Our Lord Jesus Christ

According to John's account, Jesus' ordeal begins with His arrest in the Garden of Gethsemane, near the Kidron valley. Judas, the betrayer, knows this garden well as a place Jesus has often gone with His disciples, and he maliciously leads a group of soldiers there to capture Jesus (see 18:1–11).

From the moment Jesus is arrested, He is no longer free. He becomes the property of the state, railroaded through the most fallacious, unfair, disorderly, illegal series of trials in the history of jurisprudence. No man was ever more innocent. No trials were ever more unjust.[1]

Between 2 A.M. and 7:30 A.M., Jesus is subjected to not one but six trials—three Jewish, three Roman (summarized in detail in the chart at the end of this chapter). The charge in the Jewish trials is blasphemy; but since the Jews are not allowed to administer capital punishment, they change the charge to treason. Treason, in Rome, is punishable by crucifixion. Let's look at each of these travesties in greater detail.

Trial 1

Jesus is first tried illegally during the hours of darkness at the house of Annas. Father-in-law of the high priest, Caiaphas, Annas is the wealthiest and most influential man of the city. He himself served as high priest for seventeen years and is now a sort of high priest emeritus (John 18:13). He is the power behind the throne in Jewry. And he owns and operates the entire money-changing system—the one Jesus routed in the temple courtyard. Ah, that's one event Annas has not forgotten.

With the zealous Jesus now fettered meekly before him, Annas gloatingly interrogates Him on two counts: His teaching and His disciples (v. 19). Jesus' unflinching response in verses 20–21, however, places the legal burden of proof squarely on Annas' shoulders,

---

1. According to William Barclay, the following trial laws were broken in Jesus' case: "All criminal cases must be tried during the daytime and must be completed during the daytime. Criminal cases could not be transacted during the Passover season at all. Only if the verdict was Not Guilty could a case be finished on the day it was begun; otherwise a night must elapse before the pronouncement of the verdict, so that feelings of mercy might have time to arise. . . . All evidence had to be guaranteed by two witnesses separately examined and having no contact with each other. And false witness was punishable by death." *The Gospel of Matthew*, vol. 2, rev. ed., The Daily Study Bible Series (Philadelphia, Pa.: Westminster Press, 1975), p. 353.

where it rightly belongs. The response from this impartial and fair court?

> One of the officers standing by gave Jesus a blow, saying, "Is that the way You answer the high priest?" . . . Annas therefore sent Him bound to Caiaphas the high priest. (vv. 22, 24)

Trial 2

Caiaphas is a pawn of Rome and equally corrupt but probably not as clever as Annas. Jesus is brought bound to his home in the wee hours of the night—illegalities that don't seem to bother this "priest" at all. As the ruling member of the Sanhedrin, he is responsible for ensuring a fair trial, but justice is not what he's after.

> Now the chief priests and the whole Council kept trying to obtain false testimony against Jesus, in order that they might put Him to death; and they did not find any, even though many false witnesses came forward. (Matt. 26:59–60a)

What finally breaks through their frustration is our Lord's reply to Caiaphas' point-blank interrogation in verse 63: "I adjure You by the living God, that You tell us whether You are the Christ, the Son of God." Jesus looks him in the eye and answers, "You have said it yourself" (v. 64a). With that,

> the high priest tore his robes, saying, "He has blasphemed! What further need do we have of witnesses? Behold, you have now heard the blasphemy; what do you think? They answered and said, "He is deserving of death!" Then they spat in His face and beat Him with their fists; and others slapped Him, and said, "Prophesy to us, You Christ; who is the one who hit You?" (vv. 65–68)

Trial 3

In their violent rush to judgment, the religious rulers hold a perfunctory meeting of the Sanhedrin, the supreme court of the Jews. Jurisdiction over all religious and theological matters rests here. Meeting in a place called the "council chamber," located in the Hall of Hewn Stone in the temple, it is here and only here that they can carry out official business. In probably the shortest of the six trials, lasting no more than twenty to thirty minutes, they conduct their "business" and reach their verdict.

> And when it was day, the Council of elders of the people assembled, both chief priests and scribes, and they led Him away to their council chamber, saying, "If You are the Christ, tell us." But He said to them, "If I tell you, you will not believe; and if I ask a question, you will not answer. But from now on the Son of Man will be seated at the right hand of the power of God." And they all said, "Are You the Son of God, then?" And He said to them, "Yes, I am." And they said, "What further need do we have of testimony? For we have heard it ourselves from His own mouth."
>
> Then the whole body of them arose and brought Him before Pilate. (Luke 22:66–23:1)

Trial 4

Under Roman law, the Jews are prohibited from putting someone to death, so they have to send Jesus to stand trial before the governor, Pontius Pilate. From A.D. 26 to 35, Pilate served as procurator or governor of Judea, an ill-fitting post for a man known to be sarcastic, unsympathetic, brutal—and decidedly anti-Semitic. William Barclay provides us insight into the intrigue between this man and the Jews.

> Philo, the great Jewish Alexandrian scholar, has a character study of Pilate—and Philo, remember, was not a Christian, but was speaking from the Jewish point of view. The Jews, Philo tells us, had threatened to exercise their right to report Pilate to the Emperor for his misdeeds. This threat "exasperated Pilate to the greatest possible degree, as he feared lest they might go on an embassy to the emperor, and might impeach him with respect to other particulars of his government—his corruption, his acts of insolence, his rapine, his habit of insulting people, his cruelty, his continual murders of people untried and uncondemned, and his never-ending gratuitous and most grievous inhumanity." Pilate's reputation with the Jews stank; and the fact that they could

report him made his position entirely insecure.[2]

Because of this threat, the Jews can simply turn up the thermostat and put the heat on Pilate. And now the heat is on to crucify Jesus. After a brief, bantering dialogue with the Jews (John 18:28–32), Pilate faces Jesus and asks, "Are You the King of the Jews?" (v. 33). Jesus' answer and their ensuing conversation reveal no crime of treason, so Pilate resists the flaming threat of the Jews and publicly declares Jesus innocent (vv. 34–38). But the religious rabble are still smoldering.

> They kept on insisting, saying, "He stirs up the people, teaching all over Judea, starting from Galilee, even as far as this place." (Luke 23:5)

When Pilate hears the word *Galilee*, he suddenly sees a way to cool down the simmering crowd.

Trial 5

Galilee, you see, is Herod's jurisdiction.

> When Pilate heard it, he asked whether the man was a Galilean. And when he learned that He belonged to Herod's jurisdiction, he sent Him to Herod, who himself also was in Jerusalem at that time. (vv. 6–7)

Herod Antipas, the tetrarch of Galilee, had beheaded John the Baptist (see Matt. 14:1–12). His family was notorious throughout the region: all his brothers had been murdered by their own father, and all his other relatives were also known for their iniquitous rule. Before this Herod, Jesus now stands.

> Now Herod was very glad when he saw Jesus; for he had wanted to see Him for a long time, because he had been hearing about Him and was hoping to see some sign performed by Him. And he questioned Him at some length; but He answered him nothing. And the chief priests and the scribes were standing there, accusing Him vehemently. And Herod with his soldiers, after treating Him with contempt and mocking Him, dressed Him in a gorgeous

2. Barclay, *The Gospel of Matthew*, pp. 358–59.

robe and sent Him back to Pilate. Now Herod and Pilate became friends with one another that very day; for before they had been at enmity with each other. (Luke 23:8–12)

In the face of raucous jesting and vulgar innuendoes, Jesus stands in regal dignity, silent and composed. This infuriates His enemies, who wrap a kingly robe around Him in mockery and return Him to sender—but without a verdict of guilty.

Trial 6

Again, a sharp rap on the door brings Pilate face-to-face with the enigmatic Jesus. Still worming out of any decisive action, Pilate walks the tightrope between upholding justice and placating the people by offering to rough up Jesus and then release Him (vv. 13–16). The crowd, however, isn't satisfied.

Realizing he is up against a wall, Pilate tries another route.

> Now at the feast the governor was accustomed to release for the multitude any one prisoner whom they wanted. And they were holding at that time a notorious prisoner, called Barabbas. When therefore they were gathered together, Pilate said to them, "Whom do you want me to release for you? Barabbas, or Jesus who is called Christ?" For he knew that because of envy they had delivered Him up. (Matt. 27:15–18)

Pilate gambles that this crowd, which he finds impervious to emotional appeal, will reason rationally in weighing the guilt of Barabbas, a murderer (see Mark 15:7), against the innocence of Jesus. But Pilate loses.

> The chief priests and the elders persuaded the multitudes to ask for Barabbas, and to put Jesus to death. . . . Pilate said to them, "Then what shall I do with Jesus who is called Christ?" They all said, "Let Him be crucified!" (Matt. 27:20, 22)

Matthew then tells us that Pilate "took water and washed his hands in front of the multitude, saying, 'I am innocent of this Man's blood; see to that yourselves'" (v. 24). He knew he was allowing them to shed innocent blood. Yet no matter how stubbornly he

107

washed, the stain of his decision would follow him to his grave—
a grave that would lead him face-to-face once more with the one
whose life he washed his hands of.

In a climactic finish to the final trial, Pilate addresses the crowd.

> Now it was the day of preparation for the Passover;
> it was about the sixth hour. And he said to the Jews,
> "Behold, your King!" (John 19:14)

In a crazed crescendo, the crowd announces for all eternity its
verdict.

> "Away with Him, away with Him, crucify Him!"
> Pilate said to them, "Shall I crucify your King?" The
> chief priests answered, "We have no king but Cae-
> sar." So he then delivered Him to them to be cru-
> cified. (vv. 15–16)

In our next chapter, we will walk with Jesus through the horror
of His crucifixion.

 ## Living Insights STUDY ONE

"It is safe to say," states Chuck Swindoll, "that there has never
been a more illegal, unfair, shameful set of trials conducted in the
history of jurisprudence than the six trials that led to the crucifixion
and death of the Lord Jesus Christ. . . . In this, however, there is
a paradox. *From those acts of injustice, the justice of God was satisfied.*
As men poured out their wrath on Christ at His trials and death,
God's wrath against sin was completely released upon Christ at the
cross. As a result, the only thing that now separates lost humanity
from God is unbelief. The suffering and death of Christ are now
history. He suffered and died for you. His death paid the price for
your sins. God will therefore accept you into His family today if
you will accept His offer: 'Believe on the Lord Jesus Christ, and
you will be saved' (Acts 16:31)" (emphasis added).[3]

Is unbelief standing between you and God? Perhaps you've never
thought Christ's sufferings were enough to pay the price for your

---

3. From a handout provided by Charles R. Swindoll for the First Evangelical Free Church
of Fullerton, California, March 29, 1992.

sins. Are you trying to add to them with your own penitential sufferings? Read His inviting words to you in the following verses. Let them lead you over your mountain of unbelief into His lush valley of grace and life.

John 3:16–17   1 Timothy 2:5–6

Romans 5:8   1 Peter 3:18

2 Corinthians 5:21

 Living Insights STUDY TWO

Most of us can handle the jabs that life's little hardships deliver. But how difficult it is to endure the crushing blows of injustice.

When unfair treatment blindsides us, our whole world starts spinning in a blur of inequities. Everything solid turns to sand. The legal system fails us. Longtime friends eye us with uncertainty. Then there are the inner ragings—anger steals away our sleep, thoughts of revenge sap our appetites, and doubt darkens our soul. Finally, we cry out to God like the prophet Habakkuk:

How long, O Lord, will I call for help,
And Thou wilt not hear? (1:2a)

Our questioning must inevitably lead us to the trials of Jesus. Having felt the scourge of injustice Himself, Jesus looks upon our pain and confusion with understanding eyes. All at once, we experience a depth of oneness with Him never before felt. Paul calls it "the fellowship of His sufferings" (Phil. 3:10). Instead of a list of answers, our search ends with an embrace of love.

Has injustice struck you down? In what ways do the trials of Jesus provide you with consolation and strength (see also 1 Pet. 2:20–25)?

_____

_____

_____

_____

The Trials of Jesus Christ

Trial	Officiating Authority	Scripture	Accusation	Legality	Type	Result
1	Annas, ex-high priest of the Jews (A.D. 6–15).	John 18:13–23	Trumped-up charges of irreverence to Annas.	ILLEGAL! Held at night. No specific charges. Prejudice. Violence.	Jewish and Religious	Found guilty of irreverence and rushed to Caiaphas.
2	Caiaphas—Annas' son-in-law—and the Sanhedrin (A.D. 18–36).	Matthew 26:57–68 Mark 14:53–65 John 18:24	Claiming to be the Messiah, the Son of God—blasphemy (worthy of death under Jewish law).	ILLEGAL! Held at night. False witnesses. Prejudice. Violence.	Jewish and Religious	Declared guilty of blasphemy and rushed to the Sanhedrin (Jewish supreme court).
3	The Sanhedrin—seventy ruling men of Israel (their word was needed before He could be taken to Roman officials).	Mark 15:1a Luke 22:66–71	Claiming to be the Son of God—blasphemy.	ILLEGAL! Accusation switched. No witnesses. Improper voting.	Jewish and Religious	Declared guilty of blasphemy and rushed to Roman official, Pilate.
4	Pilate, governor of Judea, who was already in "hot water" with Rome (A.D. 26–36).	Matthew 27:11–14 Mark 15:1b–5 Luke 23:1–7 John 18:28–38	Treason (accusation was changed, since treason was worthy of capital punishment in Rome).	ILLEGAL! Christ was kept under arrest, although He was found innocent. No defense attorney. Violence.	Roman and Civil	Found innocent . . . but rushed to Herod Antipas; mob overruled Pilate.
5	Herod Antipas, governor of Galilee (4 B.C.–A.D. 39).	Luke 23:8–12	No accusation was made.	ILLEGAL! No grounds. Mockery in courtroom. No defense attorney. Violence.	Roman and Civil	Mistreated and mocked; returned to Pilate without decision made by Herod.
6	Pilate (second time).	Matthew 27:15–26 Mark 15:6–15 Luke 23:18–25 John 18:39–19:16	Treason, though not proven (Pilate bargained with the mob, putting Christ on a level with Barabbas, a criminal).	ILLEGAL! Without proof of guilt, Pilate allowed an innocent man to be condemned.	Roman and Civil	Found innocent, but Pilate "washed his hands" and allowed Him to be crucified.

Chapter 12

THE AGONY OF CRUCIFIXION
Matthew 27:26–50

A gold cross, hung around your neck or pinned to your lapel, tells the world of your faith. It also symbolizes a certain morality adhered to by Christians. And wearing it often brings a degree of respect from others.

But take that tiny piece of jewelry back in time two thousand years and try wearing it around your neck or pinning it to your toga. People would give you puzzled, suspicious looks, thinking you were some kind of lunatic.

For back then, the cross was not a symbol of faith but of failure, not of morality but of lawlessness, not of respect but of unspeakable shame.

Then, the cross was not polished and esteemed. It loomed menacingly on the frayed hem of the city's outskirts, overlooking the garbage dumps. Made of rough-cut timbers and iron spikes, it stood ominously on the horizon . . . a sentry at attention, standing watch for any enemies of the empire . . . a stoic monument that crimes against the state do not pay . . . a splintered vestige of barbarism in the architecture of a renowned civilization.

For Jesus—who had no room at the inn when He was born and "nowhere to lay His head" during His life—the cross was a final place of rest. There He raised His weary, bloodstained head and asked the Judge of the universe not for vengeance, or even for justice, but for mercy on those who crucified and cursed Him. There humanity received a second chance. And an eagerly waiting Father received His Son.

That is why, for two thousand years, the cross has captured the attention of artists, poets, philosophers, and yes, even jewelers. In the cruel brutality, they've seen something beautiful; in the rough-cut wood, something golden.

This chapter has been adapted from "Death on a Cross," in the study guide *Beholding Christ . . . The Lamb of God: A Study of John 15–21*, coauthored by Ken Gire, from the Bible-teaching ministry of Charles R. Swindoll (Fullerton, Calif.: Insight for Living, 1987).

A Few Words regarding Background

In preparation for entering into the somber details of Jesus' crucifixion, let's first learn something of the prophetical and historical landscape surrounding it.

Biblical Predictions

Some people have the false impression that Jesus was a helpless victim of an insidious plot, a pitiful martyr whose plans were suddenly and unexpectedly terminated by a cross. Such was not the case at all. For more than nine centuries before He was lifted up to die, predictions of His death had been carefully preserved in the Scriptures.

Several passages in the Old Testament clearly prophesy the Messiah's crucifixion, one of the most prominent being Psalm 22. Here we see His pierced hands and feet (v. 16b), His bones pulled out of joint but not broken (vv. 14, 17), His clothing gambled for and divided (v. 18), the relentless, unmerciful mocking (vv. 7, 12–13), and His anguished cry to the Father (v. 1a).

Offering another poignant portrait of Christ's suffering is Isaiah, who describes the misery and torture of God's Servant (53:3, 5, 7, 11a), His being crucified with sinners (v. 12), and the Father's sovereign planning overarching it all (v. 10).

Historical Orientation

With the ancient prophesies ringing in our ears, we now turn to the historical setting of the Crucifixion. The first thing to notice is the time it took place. After Pilate pronounced his verdict, he delivered Jesus over to be crucified (John 19:16; Mark 15:15), which probably occurred between 7:30 and 8:00 in the morning.

The actual sentencing took place at the judgment hall located near Herod's temple. John's account helps pinpoint the place.

> When Pilate therefore heard these words, he brought Jesus out, and sat down on the judgment seat at a place called The Pavement, but in Hebrew, Gabbatha. (John 19:13)

Recent excavations have uncovered what is probably the exact site—a large, elevated, paved area at the northwest corner of the temple site that was part of the Castle Antonia. Roman soldiers were barracked there during Passover to maintain law and order.

Doubtless, they looked down from their windows as Pilate presented Jesus to the people, seeing nothing more than great sport.

A Careful Examination of the Procedure

Step by agonizing step, we'll walk with Jesus through that momentous last day of His earthly life.

The Scourging

Although it is unwarranted and unnecessary, Pilate has Jesus scourged (Matt. 27:26; Mark 15:15). There were two kinds of scourging in Jesus' day, Jewish and Roman. Jewish law specified that the victim could not receive more than forty lashes (Deut. 25:1–3). Roman law was not so humane.

> The scourging of Rome was more deadly. It was administered by a trained man, called a lictor . . . and he used a short circular piece of wood, to which were attached several strips of leather. At the end of each strip, he sewed a chunk of bone or a small piece of iron chain. This instrument was called a flagellum. There was no set number of stripes to be administered, and the law said nothing about the parts of the body to be assailed.[1]

Jesus is stripped and then tied to a low stone column. In vivid detail, historical biographer Jim Bishop re-creates the gruesome event.

> The soldier who performed flagellations for the Jerusalem garrison . . . moved to a position about six feet behind Jesus, and spread his legs. The flagellum was brought all the way back and whistled forward and made a dull drum sound as the strips of leather smashed against the back of the rib cage. The bits of bone and chain curled around the right side of the body and raised small subcutaneous hemorrhages on the chest.
> . . . The flagellum came back again, aimed slightly lower, and it crashed against skin and flesh. The lips of Jesus seemed to be moving in prayer. The

1. Jim Bishop, The Day Christ Died (New York, N.Y.: Harper and Brothers, 1957), pp. 290–91.

flagellum now moved in slow heavy rhythm.[2]

The Robe

Jesus' suffering is far from over. The cruel soldiers, who have circled around Christ's bloody body like vultures, now move in to pick at the remains.

> Then the soldiers of the governor took Jesus into the Praetorium and gathered the whole Roman cohort around Him. And they stripped Him, and put a scarlet robe on Him. (Matt. 27:27–28)

This is not a long, flowing robe. The Greek term used is *chlamus*, which signifies a short cloak worn over the shoulders. Standing there, naked from the waist down, Jesus becomes the object of their vulgar remarks.

The Crown

Then comes more violence.

> And after weaving a crown of thorns, they put it on His head, and a reed in His right hand; and they kneeled down before Him and mocked Him, saying, "Hail, King of the Jews!" And they spat on Him, and took the reed and began to beat Him on the head. And after they had mocked Him, they took His robe off and put garments on Him and led Him away to crucify Him. (vv. 29–31)

Jim Bishop again gives us insight into the scene.

> The soldier who had made the hat of thorns had gouged his fingers in doing the job. The hat was a clever piece of work because, instead of braiding a mere crown, he had fashioned it in the shape of a pileus, a Roman hat shaped in oval form, usually made of felt, which fitted like a skull cap. The dead thorns were always stacked in pails around the courtyard and were used for starting fires.[3]

Mocking, jeering, abusing—it's as if each soldier is trying to

2. Bishop, *The Day Christ Died*, p. 291.
3. Bishop, *The Day Christ Died*, p. 293.

top the other's joke. Each takes his turn spitting on Jesus . . .
cursing His name . . . slapping Him with the reed . . . punching
His raw chest with their fists. Jesus, upon whom God would soon
bestow a name that was above every other. Jesus, at whose name
every knee would someday bow, of those who are in heaven, and
on the earth, and under the earth. Jesus, before whom every tongue
would someday confess that He is Lord (Phil. 2:9–11). But for now,
humanity offers this king only spit, expletives, and fists. And Jesus
bears it all with silent, patient dignity (see 1 Pet. 2:23).

The Cross

After re-dressing Jesus, the soldiers follow their usual course
with criminals: they parade Him through town on their way to the
crucifixion site. Generally, such a victim is surrounded by four Roman soldiers and led by a centurion, all the while struggling to carry
the six-foot crossbeam that will later be attached to the larger,
vertical post of the cross. And so it is with Jesus. After the scourging
and beating, however, He is too weak to carry the beam Himself.
Matthew tells us that Simon of Cyrene is pressed into service to
help Him (27:32).

Around Christ's neck hangs a twelve by twenty-four-inch plac-
ard declaring His "crime": THIS IS JESUS THE KING OF THE JEWS
(v. 37). Pilate has had it written not only in Hebrew, so the Jews
can read it, but also in Latin for the Romans and in Greek for the
more educated and sophisticated in the crowd (John 19:20). No
one is going to miss the meaning of what's about to happen.

The Crucifixion Itself

Crucifixion was a barbaric form of capital punishment originated
in Persia. The Persians believed that the earth was sacred to Or-
muzd, the earth god, so death should not contaminate the earth.
Criminals, therefore, were fastened to vertical shafts of wood by
iron spikes and hung above the earth to die—from exposure, ex-
haustion, or suffocation. Death was painfully slow and publicly
humiliating. Cicero described crucifixion as "the most cruel and
horrifying death . . . incapable of description by any word, for
there is none fit to describe it."[4] Jim Bishop, however, again manages
to convey the horror.

4. William Barclay, *The Gospel of John*, vol. 2, rev. ed., The Daily Study Bible Series (Philadelphia, Pa.: Westminster Press, 1975), p. 250.

The executioner laid the crossbeam behind Jesus and brought him to the ground quickly by grasping his arm and pulling him backward. As soon as Jesus fell, the beam was fitted under the back of his neck and, on each side, soldiers quickly knelt on the inside of the elbows. Jesus gave no resistance and said nothing, but he groaned as he fell on the back of his head and the thorns pressed against his torn scalp.

Once begun, the matter was done quickly and efficiently. . . . With his right hand, the executioner probed the wrist of Jesus to find the little hollow spot. When he found it, he took one of the square-cut iron nails . . . raised the hammer over the nail head and brought it down with force. . . .

Two soldiers grabbed each side of the crossbeam and lifted. As they pulled up, they dragged Jesus by the wrists. With every breath, he groaned. When the soldiers reached the upright, the four of them began to lift the crossbeam higher until the feet of Jesus were off the ground. The body must have writhed with pain. . . .

When the crossbeam was set firmly, the executioner . . . knelt before the cross. Two soldiers hurried to help, and each one took hold of a leg at the calf. The ritual was to nail the right foot over the left, and this was probably the most difficult part of the work. If the feet were pulled downward, and nailed close to the foot of the cross, the prisoner always died quickly. Over the years, the Romans learned to push the feet upward on the cross, so that the condemned man could lean on the nails and stretch himself upward [to breathe].[5]

The Sign

Capping off this agonizing scene is the charge that has been placed around Jesus' neck. It, too, is nailed to the cross, as a mockery . . . yet it says more than any of them can realize (see Matt. 27:37).

5. Bishop, *The Day Christ Died*, pp. 311–12.

The Agony and Death

Excruciating pain stabs Christ's body as He hangs on unbending nails.

> The pain in his wrists was beyond bearing, and . . . muscle cramps knotted his forearms and upper arms and the pads of his shoulders; . . . his pectoral muscles at the sides of his chest were momentarily paralyzed. This induced in him an involuntary panic; for he found that while he could draw air into his lungs, he was powerless to exhale.
>
> At once, Jesus raised himself on his bleeding feet. As the weight of his body came down on the insteps, the single nail pressed hard against the top of the wound. Slowly, steadily, Jesus was forced to raise himself higher until, for the moment, his head hid the sign which told of his crime. When his shoulders were on a level with his hands, breathing was rapid and easier. . . . He fought the pain in his feet in order to breathe rapidly for a few moments. Then, unable to bear the pain below, which cramped legs and thighs and wrung moans from the strongest, he let his torso sag lower and lower, and his knees projected a little at a time until, with a deep sigh, he felt himself to be hanging by the wrists. And this process must have been repeated again and again.[6]

In every crucifixion, each movement would cut deeper into bone and tendon and raw muscle. Fever would inevitably set in, inflaming the wounds and creating an insatiable thirst. Waves of hallucinations would drift the victim in and out of consciousness. And in time, flies and other insects would find their way to the cross.

To speed up death, soldiers would break the victims' legs so they could no longer raise themselves to breathe. But with Jesus, that won't be necessary. He is already dead.

> The soldiers therefore came, and broke the legs of the first man, and of the other man who was crucified with Him; but coming to Jesus, when they saw that

---

6. Bishop, *The Day Christ Died*, p. 313.

He was already dead, they did not break His legs; but one of the soldiers pierced His side with a spear, and immediately there came out blood and water. (John 19:32–34)

One sign of death is the quick separation of dark red corpuscles from the thin, whitish serum of the blood, here called "water." Normally, the dead do not bleed. But after death, the right auricle of the human heart fills with blood, and the membrane surrounding the heart, the pericardium, holds the watery serum. Jesus' heart must have been punctured with the spear, causing both fluids to flow from His side.

The Cross and Our Hearts

Can our hearts help but be pierced too as we see the lover of our souls hanging in agony . . . for us? How can we respond to such devotion, such sacrifice? Perhaps, first, through the reverence of prayer. Quietly, slowly, read these words of Bernard of Clairvaux, then lift up your heart to the Lord.

What Thou, my Lord, hast suffered
Was all for sinners' gain;
Mine, mine was the transgression,
But Thine the deadly pain.
Lo, here I fall, my Savior;
'Tis I deserve Thy place;
Look on me with Thy favor,
Assist me with Thy grace.

What language shall I borrow
To thank Thee, dearest Friend,
For this, Thy dying sorrow,
Thy pity without end?
O make me Thine forever,
And should I fainting be,
Lord, let me never, never
Outlive my love to Thee.[7]

7. Bernard of Clairvaux, adapted by Paul Gerhardt, "O Sacred Head, Now Wounded," second and third stanzas, in The Hymnal for Worship and Celebration (Waco, Tex.: Word Music, 1986), no. 178.

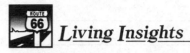

As we meditate on Christ's agonizing death and the meaning of it, we are faced with an inescapable question: What difference does His death make in my life, not just in some future, remote sense, but in the now and today I live in this moment? Author Frederick Buechner stands beside us in searching for the answer.

> He died twenty centuries ago, . . . died because in some way that he did not try to explain, his death would make all the difference, for everybody, until the end of time. Does it? Does it?
>
> It was so long ago. We do not even know what he looked like. (Or do we—would something in us recognize him if he were to appear before us?) Does that ancient death make any difference to people like us who live in a world that he could not possibly have imagined, a world of men, for many of whom God is dead? Is the death of Christ a death that really matters any more except in the dim way that any noble death might be said to matter?
>
> All I can say is that I would not be writing these words unless I believed that the answer is Yes, that his death does make all the difference, even for us. I believe that by his dying he released into the world an entirely new kind of life, his kind of life, that has flowed down through the tragic centuries like water through a dry land, making alive and whole all who will only kneel to drink. And that is the only reason why it is not blasphemy to speak of the Friday of his unspeakable death as Good Friday.[8]

Take this time to examine your own life and see what difference Christ's death has made and is making. What "entirely new kind of life" do you find in Him? What darkness has He overcome? What light has He brought you to? What does it mean to you to be God's reconciled child because of Christ?

8. Frederick Buechner, *The Hungering Dark* (New York, N.Y.: Seabury Press, 1969), pp. 109–10.

_____

_____

_____

_____

_____

_____

_____

_____

_____

_____

_____

 Living Insights

The power of Christ's cross, though we can grasp glimmers of its meaning, is so much holy mystery. You and I cannot fully fathom it, and how could our finite minds and hearts hope to; it is so vast. All of Scripture and all of life are somehow completed in our crucified Lord, as Paul wrote:

> For God has allowed us to know the secret of his plan, and it is this: he purposed long ago in his sovereign will that all human history should be consummated in Christ, that everything that exists in Heaven or earth should find its perfection and fulfilment in him. (Eph. 1:9–10 PHILLIPS)

Maybe the most we can do is live what we understand and pray the rest.

> O Thou who comest,
>   Who art the hope of the world, give us hope.
> Give us hope that beyond the worst the world can do there is such a best that not even the world can take it from us, hope that none whom thou hast loved is ever finally lost, not even to death.

O Thou who died,
　　In loneliness and pain, suffer to die in us all that keeps us from thee and from each other and from what we have it in us at our best and bravest to become. . . .

O Thou who didst rise again,
　　Thou Holy Spirit of Christ, arise and live within us now, that we may be thy body, that we may be thy feet to walk into the world's pain, thy hands to heal, thy heart to break, if need must be, for love of the world.
　　Thou risen Christ, make Christs of us all. *Amen.*[9]

9. Buechner, *The Hungering Dark*, p. 112.

Chapter 13

THE ACTS OF THE APOSTLES

Survey of Acts

Before we get rolling again on our biblical cross-country journey, we need to linger over one more place . . . Jesus' tomb. Or, more accurately, Jesus' empty tomb. For His story does not end in death on a cross but in glorious, miraculous life.

> Now after the Sabbath, as it began to dawn toward the first day of the week, Mary Magdalene and the other Mary came to look at the grave. And behold, a severe earthquake had occurred, for an angel of the Lord descended from heaven and came and rolled away the stone and sat upon it. And his appearance was like lightning, and his garment as white as snow; and the guards shook for fear of him, and became like dead men. And the angel answered and said to the women, "Do not be afraid; for I know that you are looking for Jesus who has been crucified. He is not here, for He has risen, just as He said." (Matt. 28:1–6a)

On that bright Sunday morning, with one sweep of His hand, God pushed back death's cloud and allowed the rays of hope to burst through. Jesus was alive!

In subsequent days, He appeared before His followers with several surprise visits, commissioned them to carry His flame of life to the world: "Go therefore and make disciples of all the nations" (v. 19a), but instructed them to first "stay in the city until you are clothed with power from on high" (Luke 24:49b). Then, "while He was blessing them, He parted from them" and ascended to heaven and into His Father's welcoming arms (v. 51).

As Luke closes his gospel, the disciples are in hopeful spirits. Their saga continues as Luke picks up his pen to write his sequel, The Acts of the Apostles.

Contrasts between the Gospels and Acts

Peering down the road, we can see the scenery changing as we pull out of the Gospels and head toward Acts. In the Gospels, Jesus modeled Christianity; in Acts, everyday people model Christianity. In the Gospels, the spotlight was on Christ; in Acts, His followers take center stage. The following chart explains more contrasts to watch for.

Gospels	Acts
The Son of God offers His life physically.	The Son of God offers His power spiritually.
The original "seeds" of the church are planted: "I will build My church" (Matt. 16:18).	Those seeds take root and begin to sprout, grow, bud, blossom, and bear fruit.
Christ ministers, dies, and rises from the dead.	Christ ascends, is seated and exalted as head of His Body, the church.
The emphasis rests on Jesus, the second person of the Trinity.	The emphasis rests on the Holy Spirit, the third person of the Trinity.
The events occur between about A.D. 1 and A.D. 30.	The events occur between about A.D. 30 and A.D. 60, from Christ's last words to Paul's first imprisonment.

Christ sparks the flame in the Gospels, and in Acts, His handful of followers ignite the world with that fire. The once-skeptical commentator Manford George Gutzke marveled at their amazing achievement:

His few followers were insignificant and discredited people. They faced stubborn hostility. The Jewish authorities opposed them. The Roman government opposed them and eventually came out in bitter persecution against them. . . .

Even as a skeptic, I had to admit that this Christian Gospel had tremendous strength. It became a movement and crossed every barrier. It crossed the oceans, the deserts, and the mountains. It leaped from one country to another. It spread around the world, and today it is being preached in more than a thousand different languages and dialects. From an historic point of view, Christianity is the most amazing phenomenon the world has ever seen.[1]

1. Manford George Gutzke, Plain Talk on Acts (Grand Rapids, Mich.: Zondervan Publishing House, 1966), p. 13.

Traveling through the book of Acts is bound to be a thrilling trip, so let's start the engine and get going!

Various Ways to Outline the Acts of the Apostles

Hmmm. Which route through the book shall we take? Several choices stretch before us.

Geographically

The first way to outline the book is to track Christianity's spreading flame geographically from its flash point in Jerusalem to its farthest perimeter in the world. In Acts 1:8, just before the Ascension, Jesus maps out a three-phase course for His disciples to follow:

> "You shall receive power when the Holy Spirit has come upon you; and you shall be My witnesses both in Jerusalem, and in all Judea and Samaria, and even to the remotest part of the earth."

The chapters in Acts unfold geographically according to Jesus' master plan:

- Acts 1–7:   The events in Jerusalem
- Acts 8–12:   The gospel spreads to Judea and Samaria
- Acts 13–28:   Christianity expands to "the remotest part of the earth"

Chronologically

Our second route through Acts takes us chronologically through five corridors of time marked by certain major events.

1. *The Ascension to Pentecost (chap. 1)*. The first chapter of Acts picks up where the Gospels leave off, with Jesus issuing His final words and rising into the clouds. As the awestruck disciples watch Him go, two angels appear and reassure them that their Lord "will come in just the same way as you have watched Him go into heaven" (v. 11). Comforted, the small band of believers hurries to Jerusalem and waits for the mysterious power Jesus told them would come. And come it does.

2. *Pentecost to the stoning of Stephen (chaps. 2–7)*. On the Jewish holiday of Pentecost, the believers are all together, when suddenly

there came from heaven a noise like a violent, rush-
ing wind, and it filled the whole house where they
were sitting. And there appeared to them tongues
as of fire distributing themselves, and they rested on
each one of them. (2:2–3)

Filled with the Holy Spirit, Christ's lambs rush into the streets
like lions, proclaiming Christ's death and resurrection. Miraculously,
when they open their mouths to speak, out come languages they
have never known before. All the people gathered in Jerusalem for
Pentecost are able to hear the Good News in their own tongue.
However, not everyone receives the news gladly. During this period,
the early church endures three persecutions:

- Peter and John are imprisoned (chap. 4)

- The apostles are beaten and forbidden to speak of Christ (chap. 5)

- Stephen is stoned to death—the first Christian martyr (chap. 7)

3. *Stephen's death to Saul's conversion (chaps. 8–9)*. Stephen's
shocking death sends waves of frightened Christians out of Jerusalem. On their heels is Saul, the fierce young legalist who held the
executioners' cloaks at the martyr's stoning (see 7:58). Determined
to bring these blaspheming Christians back home in chains, he sets
out for Damascus in a murderous rage. On the way, however, Jesus
appears to him in a brilliant light, saying, "Saul, Saul, why are you
persecuting Me?" (9:4). Blinded and humbled, a changed Saul ar-
rives in Damascus. After a few days, the Lord opens his eyes, showing him a new direction for his life. Saul—later called Paul—will
be Christ's principal flame-bearer to the Gentile world.

4. *Saul's conversion to the missionary journeys (chaps. 10–12)*.
Although the Lord has accepted and forgiven Saul, the Christians
fear opening their arms to this former enemy. Compassionate Barnabas, however, extends Saul his friendship, and together they become influential teachers in Antioch.

5. *The missionary journeys to Paul's imprisonment in Rome (chaps.
13–28)*. The remainder of Acts is a travelogue of Paul's four trips: three
missionary journeys and his voyage to Rome as a prisoner to stand
trial before Caesar. During this period, Paul writes thirteen letters
to various churches and individuals; these letters have been preserved
as our New Testament epistles. By reading about Paul's experiences
during his travels, we can gain rich insights into his writings.

Here is a brief itinerary of Paul's trips—you may want to follow along with the maps of his journeys in the back of your Bible.

- The first journey: Antioch, Cyprus, Pamphylia, southern Galatia, and back to Antioch (13:1–14:28)
- The second journey: return visits to Syria and Cilicia, Derbe and Lystra in Galatia; on through Asia Minor to Troas; across the Aegean Sea to Macedonia, Athens, and Corinth; and back to Antioch via Jerusalem (15:36–18:22)[2]
- The third journey: from Antioch to Ephesus, Macedonia, Greece, along the coast of Asia Minor, and to Jerusalem (18:23–21:17)[3]
- The trip to Rome: across the Mediterranean Sea to Crete, shipwrecked on Malta, on to Sicily, and finally, Rome (27:1–28:31)[4]

Biographically

A third way to tour Acts focuses on the book's two most prominent figures: Peter—chapters 1 through 12, and Paul—chapters 13 through 28. When we divide the book like this, some fascinating contrasts emerge between the two sections.

Peter *Acts 1–12*	Paul *Acts 13–28*
Central location: Jerusalem	Central location: Antioch
Emphasis on Jews	Emphasis on Gentiles
Movement from Jerusalem to Samaria	Movement from Samaria to Rome
Five great persecutions	Four great journeys
Period of refinement	Period of fulfillment

Several Firsts in the Book of Acts

Traveling through Acts reminds us of our trip through Genesis back in chapter 4. In many ways, Genesis is to the Old Testament

2. During Paul's second journey, he wrote 1 and 2 Thessalonians.

3. During Paul's third journey, he wrote 1 and 2 Corinthians, Galatians, and Romans. (According to some scholars, however, Paul wrote Galatians earlier, just after his first journey.)

4. While in Rome, Paul penned the Prison Epistles. During his first imprisonment, he wrote Ephesians, Philippians, Colossians, and Philemon. During his second imprisonment, soon before his execution, he wrote 1 and 2 Timothy and Titus.

what Acts is to the New Testament—both are the seedbeds in which several key biblical themes get their start. For example, the Hebrew nation begins with Abraham in Genesis and branches out into subsequent Old Testament books. Likewise, some of the many firsts in Acts bear fruit in the rest of the New Testament. In Acts we find:

- The first permanent indwelling of the Holy Spirit and the beginning of Christ's universal church (chap. 2)[5]

- The first formation of local assemblies of believers (chaps. 2–4)

- The first act of church discipline (chap. 5)

- The first organization of church government (chap. 6)

- The first martyr (chap. 7)

- The first missionary: Philip (chap. 8)

- The first time the gospel is delivered to Gentiles: Peter and Cornelius (chap. 10)

- The first use of the name *Christians* (11:26)

- The first organized approach to world evangelism (chaps. 13–28)

Trace the vital New Testament concepts to their roots, and you'll soon be digging up the stories of people, events, and ideas found in the book of Acts. For that reason, it's important to keep in mind three facts while reading this book.

Three Valuable Facts to Remember about Acts

First, *because many of the people mentioned in the New Testament are introduced in Acts, get acquainted with them here.* Get to know Mark and Timothy and James, not just Paul and Peter. You'll read the Bible with much greater interest if its characters are your familiar friends.

Second, *since most of the events that pertain to the church are*

---

5. In the Old Testament, the Holy Spirit temporarily indwelled certain people to do special tasks for God. For example, when the Spirit came upon Samson, he could perform mighty acts of strength (see Judg. 15:14–15). At any time, the Spirit could leave a person, such as the time He departed from King Saul, never to return (see 1 Sam. 16:14). However, in the New Testament, the Spirit indwells people permanently and seals their salvation the moment they believe in Christ (see Eph. 1:13–14).

recorded in Acts, become a student of them here. Reading Philippians, for instance, will take on a whole new meaning if you first know what happened to Paul in Philippi (see Acts 16).

Third, because many of the truths addressed later in the Epistles find their origins in Acts, familiarize yourself with them here. The great creeds of the church and those wonderful doctrines into which we sink our theological roots begin right here, in the book of Acts.

 Living Insights STUDY ONE

Persecution has never held back the church. On the contrary, fierce storms drive the ship onward. The day Stephen was killed, a great persecution launched the believers from their dock in Jerusalem. As a result, a church was established in Antioch and became the hub for Gentile outreach. From there, Paul sailed through Asia and Europe, propelled by the howling winds of persecution. Eventually, the oppression forced him as far as Rome. But even while under arrest, he kept on

> preaching the kingdom of God, and teaching con-
> cerning the Lord Jesus Christ with all openness, un-
> hindered. (Acts 28:31)

Unhindered. The word unfurls like a banner at the end of the book. Nothing could restrain the church, neither threats nor beatings nor prison walls.

Today, rancorous people and evil forces still try to shipwreck the church and its gospel message. Have you felt those forces in your life? What confidence does the story of Acts give you to face these storms and keep on sharing the kingdom of God "with all openness, unhindered?"

_____

_____

_____

_____

_____

_____

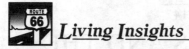

Living Insights

What a whirlwind tour of Acts! To help nail down what you've learned before it blows away from your memory, take time to review some of the people, places, and events you've become acquainted with in this exciting book.

If I wanted to spend time with . . .	I would go to chapter(s) . . .
Stephen	_____
Philip	_____
Paul on his first journey	_____
the newly Spirit-filled disciple	_____
Peter and Cornelius	_____
Jesus before He ascended	_____

If I wanted to visit . . .	I would travel through chapter(s) . . .
Rome	_____
Jerusalem	_____
the Damascus Road	_____
Judea and Samaria	_____

If I wanted to learn about . . .	I would study chapter(s) . . .
Pentecost	_____
the first church discipline	_____
salvation extended to Gentiles	_____
the formation of church government	_____

Chapter 14

THE LETTERS AND THE LAST PROPHECY

Survey of Romans through Revelation

Welcome to California!"
For carloads of Route 66 travelers heading west, seeing that sign on the side of the road always brought cheers and visions of swaying palms and foamy beaches. Between them and paradise, however, lay the forbidding Mojave Desert and a string of hobo towns like Needles, Essex, and Amboy. Beyond them stood the San Bernardino Mountains rising up like soldiers guarding the City of Angels. Pilgrims to this promised land had to struggle to the summit, but once through the Cajon Pass, they felt like they were at the top of the world. At dusk, the sprawling Los Angeles basin resembled a sea of sparkling city lights, all flowing into a golden setting sun.

As we approach the end of God's Route 66, the remaining twenty-two books of the Bible appear like those city lights. Each one of them shimmers with promise and points to the Bible's glowing Son, Jesus Christ. With our eyes on Him, let's drive through the rest of the New Testament, anticipating the final destination of our long journey.

Ways to Categorize the Final Books

Our route through the Epistles and Revelation might follow any of three trails. We can journey through the books following the writers, the recipients, or the content.

According to the Writer

Thirteen of these letters were written by the apostle Paul— fourteen if he was the unidentified author of Hebrews.[1]

---

1. Who wrote Hebrews is a mystery yet to be solved. According to the earliest tradition, Paul is the author. However, the style of writing in Hebrews is different from Paul's other books. Another early tradition suggests Barnabas because of his levitical background (see Acts 4:36), but this cannot be proven. Scholars have argued for other authors, including Clement of Rome, Luke, Silvanus, Philip the Evangelist, Priscilla, and Apollos. In the end, only God knows the writer of Hebrews. For a fuller discussion, see Zane C. Hodges, "Hebrews," in The Bible Knowledge Commentary, New Testament ed., ed. John F. Walvoord and Roy B. Zuck (Wheaton, Ill.: Scripture Press Publications, Victor Books, 1983), pp. 777–78.

- Romans
- 1 and 2 Corinthians
- Galatians
- Ephesians
- Philippians

- Colossians
- 1 and 2 Thessalonians
- 1 and 2 Timothy
- Titus
- Philemon

John penned four books: three letters—1, 2, and 3 John—and the book of Revelation. Peter authored two: 1 and 2 Peter. James, the brother of Jesus, wrote one book, and Jude wrote one as well.

According to the Recipient

Most of the books were written as letters to *churches* in certain cities or regions, such as Rome, Corinth, Galatia, Ephesus, Philippi, Colossae, and Thessalonica.

A second set of books was addressed to *individuals*: Timothy, Titus, Philemon, and John's friends—"the chosen lady and her children" (2 John 1) and Gaius (3 John).

The third group includes the books composed for *Christians in general*. These are Hebrews, James, 1 and 2 Peter, 1 John, Jude, and Revelation.

According to the Content

This last course takes us down the road of content. By clustering the books according to their overall subject matter, we can identify four general categories.

Christian Doctrine	Romans, Galatians, Ephesians, Colossians, Hebrews, 2 Peter, and 1 John
Practical Advice	1 Corinthians, Philippians, 1 and 2 Thessalonians, 1 Peter, James, and 2 John
Pastoral Matters/Church Counsel	1 and 2 Timothy and Titus (often called the Pastoral Epistles)
Personal Matters	2 Corinthians, Philemon, 3 John, and Jude

While we're shuffling the books around, let's arrange them one other way—according to when they were written.

Chronology and Overview of These Books

The table of contents in our Bibles lists the Pauline Epistles first, beginning with Romans and ending with Philemon. Then it lists the General Epistles from Hebrews through Jude, crowning the New Testament with the book of Revelation. However, this is not their chronological order. If we listed them from the earliest to the latest, the sequence would look like this:

1. James	9. Philemon	16. 2 Peter
2. 1 Thessalonians	10. Ephesians	17. Jude
3. 2 Thessalonians	11. Philippians	18. Hebrews
4. 1 Corinthians	12. 1 Timothy	19. 1 John
5. 2 Corinthians	13. Titus	20. 2 John
6. Galatians	14. 2 Timothy	21. 3 John
7. Romans	15. 1 Peter	22. Revelation
8. Colossians		

However, since we're more accustomed to the way in which they appear in our Bibles, let's visit them in that order with a few brief comments as we drive by each one on our way to Revelation.

- **Romans**—written while Paul was in the debauched city of Corinth; the most significant statement of Christian doctrine in the Bible.

- **1 Corinthians**—corrects a number of problems in the local church in Corinth.

- **2 Corinthians**—a very personal letter from Paul to the Corinthian believers defending himself as an apostle; includes one of the most helpful sections on financial giving.

- **Galatians**—draws Christians away from legalism into the liberty of God's grace.

- **Ephesians**—highlights our position as believers in Christ and our ministry to one another as members of His body; includes a section on the Christian's spiritual armor.

- **Philippians**—portrays the genuine joy available to us in spite of our circumstances.

- **Colossians**—spotlights the greatness of Christ as the exalted Head of the church.

- **1 Thessalonians**—an excellent tutor for new believers to learn about the Christian life and the church; includes lots of practical truths.

- **2 Thessalonians**—encourages persecuted believers and provides a great section on future events.

- **1 Timothy**—a "how-to" book for the local church; makes a good manual for pastors and congregations to follow.

- **2 Timothy**—records Paul's touching last words before his death; written from a dungeon.

- **Titus**—echoes 1 Timothy's instructions about local church organization.

- **Philemon**—letter to a slave owner to convince him to welcome back his runaway slave, Onesimus, who recently became a Christian.

- **Hebrews**—addresses the Jewish converts to Christianity, many of whom wanted to return to Judaism because they weren't sure faith in Christ alone could please God; teaches that Christ is superior to the Law and points to the many symbols of Christ in the Old Testament.

- **James**—the "Proverbs" of the New Testament; full of sound, straightforward advice about living out the truths Christ taught.

- **1 Peter**—describes the ways Christians should react to suffering.

- **2 Peter**—warns believers how to spot money-hungry false teachers in the church.

- **1 John**—underscores fellowship and the importance of believers getting along well with God and others.

- **2 John**—John's personal letter to an unidentified lady and her children; helps us know how to handle false teachers in the church.

- **3 John**—a letter of encouragement to the church leader Gaius; mentions two other men, Diotrephes and Demetrius.

- **Jude**—a letter of warning, like 2 Peter; we could call it "the Acts of the Apostates."

- **Revelation**—unveils God's plan for the future; includes His judgments, the Tribulation, Christ's return, the millennial kingdom, and heaven.

With the book of Revelation, our Route 66 comes to an end. But its story lives on. John's revelation of the future, like the Pacific Ocean, stretches out as far as the eye can see. Enlivened by the crisp salt breeze, we pause to admire the sun as its colors flood the sky and dance on the water. The Morning Star. He set us on our journey in the east, and now He meets us in the west; Christ is indeed the sunrise and sunset of Scripture—and our lives. Commentator John Walvoord reminds us of Christ's overarching role:

> In earlier books of the Bible, Christ is introduced in the Messianic prophecies and the activities of the Angel of Jehovah in the Old Testament. The revelation of Jesus Christ is advanced in the Gospels and the Acts, which unfold the birth, life, ministry, death, resurrection, and ascension of the Son of God. The epistles add the theological interpretation of the person and work of Christ. To all of this dramatic and tremendously significant revelation, the last book of the Bible provides the capstone. It is indeed "the revelation of Jesus Christ" not only as the Lamb that was slain, a familiar portrayal in the book, but as King of kings and Lord of lords who is certain to return to the earth in power and glory to judge the wicked and reward the righteous.[2]

Many times, though, we are afraid to enter this mysterious book to behold Christ in His glory. Perhaps the enigmatic symbols intimidate us. Maybe we assume we cannot understand the book anyway, so why try? Possibly we fear becoming fanatical about future things, going off the prophetical "deep end." Or our hesitance may be a by-product of Satan's goal to veil the truth from our eyes— particularly the truth about his eventual destruction in the lake of fire (see Rev. 20:1–10).

Don't let these things dampen your enthusiasm to know Christ in Revelation or any other part of Scripture. He is waiting to meet you here, the Light of the universe, the One of whom the heavenly creatures will one day sing:

> "Worthy is the Lamb that was slain to receive power and riches and wisdom and might and honor and glory and blessing." . . . "To Him who sits on the

---

2. John F. Walvoord, *The Revelation of Jesus Christ* (Chicago, Ill.: Moody Press, 1966), p. 7.

throne, and to the Lamb, be blessing and honor and glory and dominion forever and ever." (Rev. 5:12, 13b)

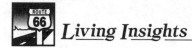 *Living Insights*   STUDY ONE

Like lights in a dark sky, the final books of the Bible guide us in many ways:

- They clarify the details of living the Christian life—how to be saved and then walk in the Spirit, how to pray and grow into mature believers.

- They establish primary principles of the faith—worship, church government, spiritual gifts, missions, the great doctrines of redemption, atonement, sanctification, and many more.

- They give us the clearest view of the future—the Rapture, the Tribulation, the Millennium, the glorious rule of Christ.

Imagine how difficult it would be to grope through the Christian life without these twenty-two guiding lamps. At the death of a loved one, we would feel lost on a sea of grief without Paul's reassuring beacon of truth in 1 Thessalonians:

> But we do not want you to be uninformed, brethren, about those who are asleep, that you may not grieve, as do the rest who have no hope. For if we believe that Jesus died and rose again, even so God will bring with Him those who have fallen asleep in Jesus. (4:13–14)

To review some of the other ways the Epistles and Revelation shine a light on our lives, jot down in the column on the right the name of the book or books that correspond with the issue we've listed on the left.

If I am . . .   **Then I'll find guidance in . . .**
suffering   _____
lacking joy   _____
needing fellowship   _____
confined by legalism   _____
leading the church   _____

Are you drifting in the dark about a certain area of your Christian life? If so, write down the issue you're struggling with and the name of the book that will light the way for you. Then make a plan to read that book in the weeks ahead.

_____

_____

_____

 Living Insights

We sure have come a long way! Can you remember the course we mapped out on the Route 66 diagram way back in chapter 1? Here's another way to illustrate the sixty-six books and their categories.

THE BIBLE

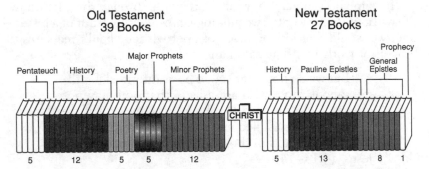

Old Testament
39 Books

New Testament
27 Books

Pentateuch   History   Poetry   Major Prophets   Minor Prophets   History   Pauline Epistles   General Epistles   Prophecy

CHRIST

5   12   5   5   12   5   13   8   1

After any trip, it's a good idea to organize your photos in an album right away while your memory is fresh. To help you paste down in your mind the snapshots you took traveling through the New Testament, circle the correct answers on this short quiz.[3]

1. Matthew's gospel portrays Christ as
   a. a mighty king
   b. a brave warrior
   c. a soaring eagle

3. The answers are provided after the "Books for Probing Further" section at the end of the guide.

2. Mark's gospel pictures Christ as
   a. a mild dove
   b. a humble servant
   c. a wise teacher

3. Luke's gospel shows Christ as
   a. an ideal man
   b. the Great Physician
   c. a shining angel

4. John's gospel reveals Christ as
   a. a gentle shepherd
   b. the Great Fisherman
   c. the Son of God

5. Which of the following events do the Gospels reveal about Christ?
   a. His existence before time began
   b. His coming and living among humanity
   c. His suffering and death in our place
   d. His resurrection and ascension
   e. His return as ruler of the earth
   f. all of the above

6. How many trials did Christ endure?
   a. two
   b. six
   c. four

7. How long did Jesus suffer on the cross?
   a. three hours
   b. one day
   c. six hours

8. Which of the following ways can we outline the book of Acts?
   a. geographically
   b. ideologically
   c. numerically

9. Which are the Pastoral Epistles?
   a. Romans, 1 Corinthians, Jude, Revelation
   b. 1 and 2 Timothy, Titus
   c. Philippians, Philemon, 1 and 2 Peter

10. Who wrote Revelation?
    a. Jesus Christ
    b. John the Baptist
    c. the apostle John

◆

A Parting Word

Congratulations! It took a lot of stick-to-itiveness to travel all the way from Genesis to Revelation. And you made it! We applaud your diligence. But it doesn't have to end here, you know. May our journey together be only the beginning of your lifelong love affair with the Road—God's Route 66.

BOOKS FOR
PROBING FURTHER

To guide you on your future travels along God's Route 66, we've compiled a few resources you may wish to carry along. *Happy motoring!*

Anders, Max E. *30 Days to Understanding the Bible*. Brentwood, Tenn.: Wolgemuth and Hyatt, Publishers, 1988.

Baxter, J. Sidlow. *Explore the Book*. Grand Rapids, Mich.: Zondervan Publishing House, Academie Books, 1960.

Green, Joel B. *How to Read the Gospels and Acts*. Downers Grove, Ill.: InterVarsity Press, 1987.

Scroggie, W. Graham. *A Guide to the Gospels*. 1948. Reprint, London, England: Pickering and Inglis, 1965.

Stedman, Ray C. *Highlights of the Bible: Poets and Prophets*. Ventura, Calif.: Regal Books, 1981.

Stott, John R. W. *Understanding the Bible*. Revised edition. Grand Rapids, Mich.: Zondervan Publishing House, 1984.

Tenney, Merrill C. *New Testament Survey*. Revised edition. Grand Rapids, Mich.: William B. Eerdmans Publishing Co., 1961.

———. *New Testament Times*. Grand Rapids, Mich.: William B. Eerdmans Publishing Co., 1965.

Wilkinson, Bruce, and Kenneth Boa. *Talk Thru the Bible*. Nashville, Tenn.: Thomas Nelson Publishers, 1983.

Some of the books listed above may be out of print and available only through a library. For those currently available, please contact your local Christian bookstore. Books by Charles R. Swindoll are available through Insight for Living. IFL also offers some books by other authors—please note the ordering information that follows and contact the office that serves you.

1. beginnings
2. any of the following: Creation, Fall, Flood, Babel, birth of the nations
3. any of the following: Adam, Eve, Cain, Abel, Enoch, Noah, Abraham, Sarah, Lot, Isaac, Rebekah, Esau, Jacob, Rachel, Joseph
4. Exodus
5. Leviticus
6. wanderings
7. Deuteronomy
8. Joshua
9. Judges
10. Ruth
11. united
12. Saul, David, Solomon
13. Job, Psalms, Proverbs, Ecclesiastes, Song of Solomon
14. divided
15. northern kingdom: Israel; southern kingdom: Judah
16. Hosea
17. Assyrians
18. Babylonians
19. Ezekiel, Daniel
20. Nehemiah
21. four hundred years

Answers to Chapter 14 New Testament Review

1. (a) a mighty king
2. (b) a humble servant
3. (a) an ideal man
4. (c) the Son of God
5. (f) all of the above
6. (b) six
7. (c) six hours
8. (a) geographically
9. (b) 1 and 2 Timothy, Titus
10. (c) the apostle John

ORDERING INFORMATION

A LOOK AT THE BOOK

Cassette Tapes and Study Guide

This Bible study guide was designed to be used independently or in conjunction with the broadcast of Chuck Swindoll's taped messages which are listed below. If you would like to order cassette tapes or further copies of this study guide, please see the information given below and the order forms provided at the end of this guide.

		U.S.	Canada
LAB	Study guide	— $ 4.95 ea.	$ 6.50 ea.
LABCS	Cassette series, includes all individual tapes, album cover, and one complimentary study guide	48.85	62.00
LAB 1–7	Individual cassettes, includes messages A and B	6.30 ea.	8.00 ea.

The prices are subject to change without notice.

LAB 1-A: *Three Gates That Open the Scriptures*—Selected Scriptures
B: *A Look at the Book*—Selected Scriptures

LAB 2-A: *The Flow of Biblical History: His Story*—Selected Scriptures
B: *From Creation to a Nation*—Survey of Genesis through Deuteronomy

LAB 3-A: *The Rise of the Hebrew Nation*—Survey of Joshua through 2 Samuel
B: *The Decline and Fall of the Hebrew Nation*—Survey of 1 Kings through 2 Chronicles

LAB 4-A: *The Books of Poetry*—Survey of Job through Song of Solomon
B: *Those Grand Old Books of Prophecy*—Survey of Isaiah through Malachi

LAB 5-A: *Four Centuries of Silence*—Daniel 2:31–33, 36–40; 7:1–8
B: *Why Four Gospels?*—Survey of the Gospels

141

LAB   6-A: *A Closer Look at Jesus' Arrest and Trials*—Selected
      Scriptures
      B: *The Agony of Crucifixion*—Matthew 27:26–50

LAB   7-A: *The Acts of the Apostles*—Survey of Acts
      B: *The Letters and the Last Prophecy*—Survey of Romans
      through Revelation

How to Order by Phone or FAX

(Credit card orders only)

United States: 1-800-772-8888 from 7:00 A.M. to 4:30 P.M., Pacific time,
      Monday through Friday
      FAX (714) 575-5496 anytime, day or night

Canada: 1-800-663-7639, Vancouver residents call (604) 596-2910 from
7:00 A.M. to 5:00 P.M., Pacific time, Monday through Friday
FAX (604) 596-2975 anytime, day or night

Australia: (03) 872-4606 or FAX (03) 874-8890 from 9:00 A.M. to
      5:00 P.M., Monday through Friday

Other International Locations: call the Ordering Services Department in
the United States at (714) 575-5000 during the hours listed above.

How to Order by Mail

United States
• Mail to: Ordering Services Department
      Insight for Living
      Post Office Box 69000
      Anaheim, CA 92817-0900
• Sales tax: California residents add 7.25%.
• Shipping: add 10% of the total order amount for first-class delivery.
(Otherwise, allow four to six weeks for fourth-class delivery.)
• Payment: personal checks, money orders, credit cards (Visa, MasterCard,
Discover Card, and American Express). No invoices or COD orders available.
• $10 fee for *any* returned check.

Canada
- Mail to: Insight for Living Ministries
  Post Office Box 2510
  Vancouver, BC V6B 3W7
- Sales tax: please add 7% GST. British Columbia residents also add 7% sales tax (on tapes or cassette series).
- Shipping: included in prices listed above.
- Payment: personal checks, money orders, credit cards (Visa, Master-Card). No invoices or COD orders available.
- Delivery: approximately four weeks.

Australia, New Zealand, or Papua New Guinea
- Mail to: Insight for Living, Inc.
  GPO Box 2823 EE
  Melbourne, Victoria 3001, Australia
- Shipping and delivery time: please see chart that follows.
- Payment: personal checks payable in U.S. funds, international money orders, or credit cards (Visa, MasterCard).

Other International Locations
- Mail to: Ordering Services Department
  Insight for Living
  Post Office Box 69000
  Anaheim, CA 92817-0900
- Shipping and delivery time: please see chart that follows.
- Payment: personal checks payable in U.S. funds, international money orders, or credit cards (Visa, MasterCard, and American Express).

Type of Shipping	Postage Cost	Delivery
Surface	10% of total order*	6 to 10 weeks
Airmail	25% of total order*	under 6 weeks

Use U.S. price as a base.

Our Guarantee

Your complete satisfaction is our top priority here at Insight for Living. If you're not completely satisfied with anything you order, please return it for full credit, a refund, or a replacement, as you prefer.

Insight for Living Catalog

The Insight for Living catalog features study guides, tapes, and books by a variety of Christian authors. To obtain a free copy, call us at the numbers listed above.

Order Form
United States, Australia, and Other International Locations
(Canadian residents please use order form on reverse side.)

LABCS represents the entire *A Look at the Book* series in a special album cover, while LAB 1–7 are the individual tapes included in the series. LAB represents this study guide, should you desire to order additional copies.

LAB	Study guide	$ 4.95 ea.
LABCS	Cassette series, includes all individual tapes, album cover, and one complimentary study guide	48.85
LAB 1–7	Individual cassettes, includes messages A and B	6.30 ea.

Product Code	Product Description	Quantity	Unit Price	Total
			$	$
		Subtotal		
	California Residents—Sales Tax *Add 7.25% of subtotal.*			
	U.S. First-Class Shipping *For faster delivery, add 10% for postage and handling.*			
	Non-United States Residents *U.S. price plus 10% surface postage or 25% airmail.*			
	Gift to Insight for Living *Tax-deductible in the United States.*			
	Total Amount Due *Please do not send cash.*		$	

Prices are subject to change without notice.

Payment by: ❑ Check or money order payable to Insight for Living   ❑ Credit card

(Circle one):   Visa   MasterCard   Discover Card   American Express

Number _____

Expiration Date _____   Signature _____
We cannot process your credit card purchase without your signature.

Name _____

Address _____

City _____   State _____

Zip Code _____   Country _____

Telephone (____) _____   Radio Station ____ ____ ____ ____
If questions arise concerning your order, we may need to contact you.

Mail this order form to the Ordering Services Department at one of these addresses:

Insight for Living
Post Office Box 69000, Anaheim, CA 92817-0900

Insight for Living, Inc.
GPO Box 2823 EE, Melbourne, VIC 3001, Australia

ECFA MEMBER

Order Form
Canadian Residents

(Residents of the United States, Australia, and other international locations,
please use order form on reverse side.)

LABCS represents the entire *A Look at the Book* series in a special album cover, while LAB
1–7 are the individual tapes included in the series. LAB represents this study guide, should
you desire to order additional copies.

LAB	Study guide	$ 6.50 ea.
LABCS	Cassette series,	62.00
	includes all individual tapes, album cover,	
	and one complimentary study guide	
LAB 1–7	Individual cassettes,	8.00 ea.
	includes messages A and B	

Product Code	Product Description	Quantity	Unit Price	Total
			$	$
			Subtotal	
			Add 7% GST	
		British Columbia Residents *Add 7% sales tax on individual tapes or cassette series.*		
		Gift to Insight for Living Ministries *Tax-deductible in Canada.*		
		Total Amount Due *Please do not send cash.*		$

Prices are subject to change without notice.

Payment by: ☐ Check or money order payable to Insight for Living Ministries
☐ Credit card

(Circle one): Visa   MasterCard   Number _____

Expiration Date _____   Signature _____
We cannot process your credit card purchase without your signature.

Name _____

Address _____

City _____   Province _____

Postal Code _____   Country _____

Telephone (____) _____   Radio Station ____ ____ ____ ____
If questions arise concerning your order, we may need to contact you.

Mail this order form to the Ordering Services Department at the following address:

Insight for Living Ministries
Post Office Box 2510
Vancouver, BC, Canada V6B 3W7